Welsh Thousand Foot Challenges

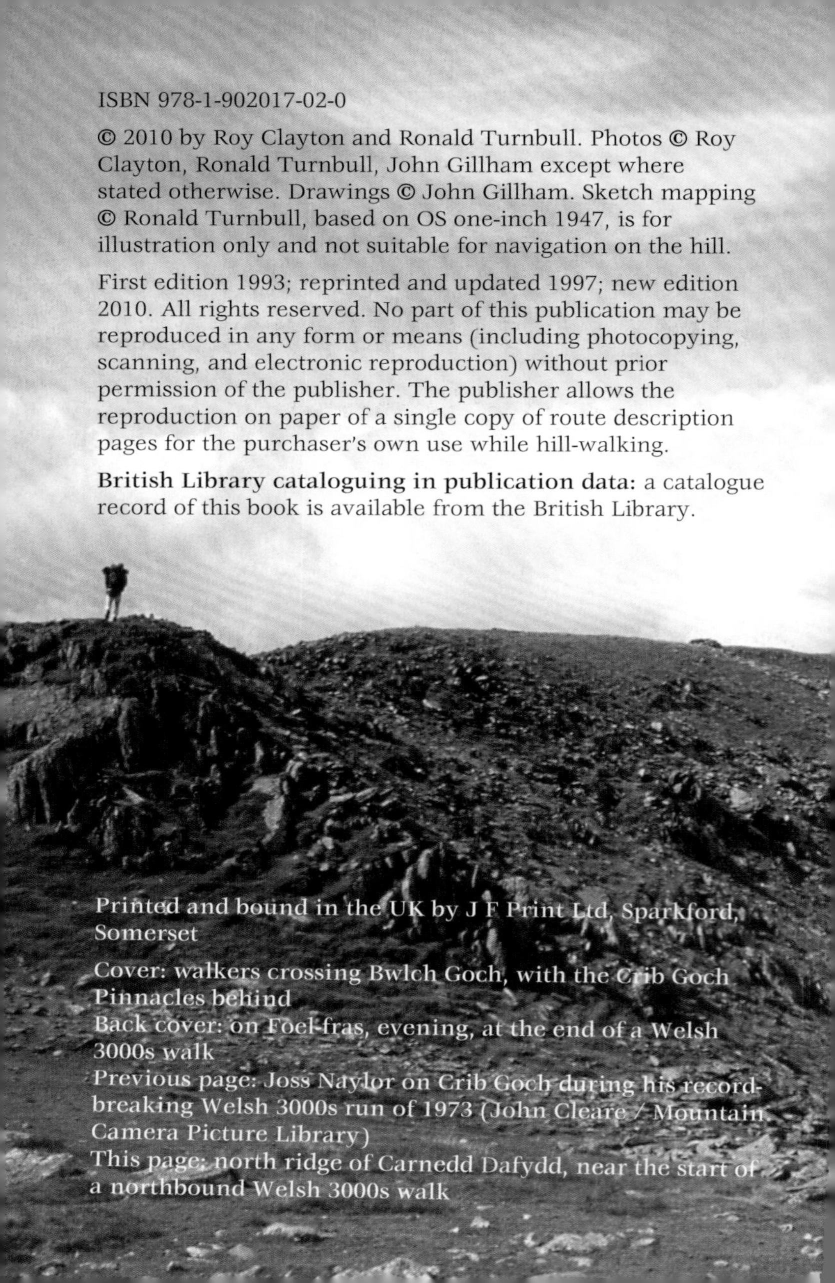

ISBN 978-1-902017-02-0

First edition 1993; reprinted and updated 1997; new edition 2010.

British Library cataloguing in publication data: a catalogue record of this book is available from the British Library.

Printed and bound in the UK by J F Print Ltd, Sparkford, Somerset

Cover: walkers crossing Bwlch Goch, with the Crib Goch Pinnacles behind
Back cover: on Foel-fras, evening, at the end of a Welsh 3000s walk
Previous page: Joss Naylor on Crib Goch during his record-breaking Welsh 3000s run of 1973 (John Cleare / Mountain Camera Picture Library)
This page: north ridge of Carnedd Dafydd, near the start of a northbound Welsh 3000s walk

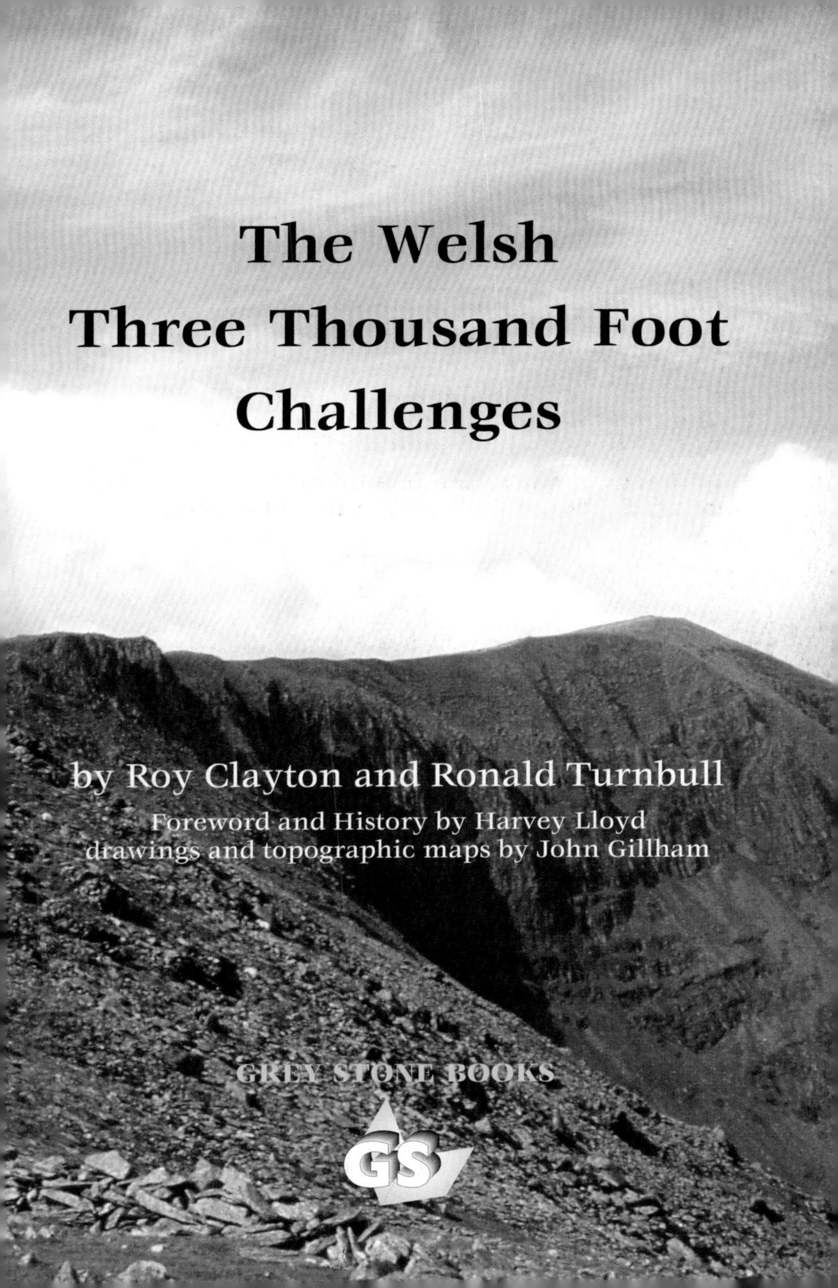

The Welsh Three Thousand Foot Challenges

by Roy Clayton and Ronald Turnbull

Foreword and History by Harvey Lloyd
drawings and topographic maps by John Gillham

GREY STONE BOOKS

GS

Also by Roy Clayton and Ronald Turnbull:
Lakeland Mountain Challenges (Grey Stone Books, 1999, updating 2010)

Also by Ronald Turnbull:
Across Scotland on Foot (Grey Stone Books)
Long Days in Lakeland (Grey Stone Books)
Three Peaks Ten Tors – Long-distance and Challenge Walks in the UK (Cicerone Press)
Granite & Grit – a hillwalkers guide to the UK's mountain geology (Frances Lincoln)
www.ronaldturnbull.co.uk

Acknowledgments

We thank those who have helped us in the preparation of this book: Harvey Lloyd, who has been a major source of detailed knowledge of the area; Colin Donnelly for photos and accounts of his Welsh 3000s record; James Clayton, Janet Smith, Peter Branthwaite, Glyn Jones, Colin Brash and Nicola Gillham for their company on the hills; Ken Vickers for his invaluable advice; Ian Waddell for creating the unique Dragon's Back Race as well as information and photos of it; Depot Para, Aldershot (the Parachute Regiment) for food and shelter on the Dragon's Back; John Cleare for his inspiring photos of Joss Naylor; and John Gillham for his drawings, hill knowledge, support and encouragement and also for car support on the Paddy Buckley Round.

www.grey-stone.co.uk

CONTENTS

Foreword

by Harvey Lloyd

Former warden of Pen y Pass (Gorphwysfa) Youth Hostel and organiser of the Welsh 1000 Metres Race, and the man who in 1973 saved the Cromlech Boulders from planned road widening in Llanberis Pass

My foreword could begin like a child's story. "Once upon a time there was a man named E.G. Rowland, who liked to walk amongst the Welsh Hills and decided to write a book called *Hill Walking in Snowdonia ...*"

E.G. Rowland was one of the people who introduced me to the region over fifty years ago – fifty years that have brought to me the most wonderful experiences. Known even then as "the old man of the mountains", the written words of this veteran rambler and mountaineer became part of the motivation and inspiration leading to the upturn in interest in hill walking in the fifties.

Up until the mid nineties I was youth hostel warden at Pen y Pass and lived amongst these glorious mountains. I was delighted when approached by Roy Clayton to help with this book. In putting it together Roy, Ronald Turnbull and myself hope that it will spread the call of the mountains to a wider public.

My first attempt at the Welsh Three Thousands took place on a Sunday in June. At 5am I am never at my best and peering into a cloudy environment crisscrossed with the beams of head-torches was not encouraging for a novice of long mountain treks. I was accompanied by a group of experienced mountain people, however, and I had worked at getting fit. It was a case of head down and hope for better weather later in the day. Luck was with us and we came through the cloud on Crib Goch – the cotton wool layer below extending towards Anglesey and the Irish Sea. The sun warmed our cold limbs. Suddenly Snowdon was a wonderful place to be.

The day progressed well. Support groups in Nant Peris and Ogwen supplied much needed sustenance. The traverse of the Carneddau was highlighted by a glorious setting sun, diluting the pain and fatigue that the day's rigours had brought about.

The next attempt was quite different. The day again started wet and miserable but the traverse of Crib Goch, Carnedd Ugain and Snowdon passed reasonably well. The trouble started on the descent to Nant Peris. A bad choice of route and laziness in not consulting a compass, brought us to very steep ground above Cwm Glas Bach and delayed our arrival in the village until late morning. The weather continued to deteriorate and morale was low. The Glyders were very wet and the attempt was aborted at Ogwen. We learned from our foolishness. A compass in the rucksack does not help in route finding, even in the hills we thought we knew so well!

Finally a word about conservation of the environment over which we travel. The National Parks are managed to promote "quiet enjoyment" for the population. Headlines such as "Charity runners threaten Snowdon" in the newspapers suggest an increased resistance to any sort of organised event. The land in the Snowdonia National Park is largely privately owned and the route crosses several ecologically sensitive sites – Snowdonia is well known for its rare alpine plants. In addition to this local farmers are finding it increasingly difficult to make a living from rearing sheep on such hostile terrain. The problems have been made worse by the increasing numbers of walkers and it is important that everybody should be concerned to protect this fragile region. Always follow the Country Code and be considerate to landowners, residents and other land users.

The popularity of the Welsh 3's has been firmly established. The greats will continue to work at knocking minutes off existing records; the also-rans will try to better their previous times and the mountains will always be there for anyone, whether rich or poor – to walk over, to run over or simply to admire from the comfort of valley or village.

Harvey Lloyd, Nant Gwynant

Y Lliwedd from Yr Wyddfa's east ridge

Introduction to the first edition

Snowdon, Tryfan, Crib Goch: names to stir the blood - and bootsoles - of any mountain man or woman... My first acquaintance with these peaks was on one of those whistle-stop coach tours. The driver proudly pointed out the peaks of Snowdon, the principality's highest mountain, but my senses were more stirred by the rugged ramparts of the Glyder range on the other side of the coach. Later in the day, standing on the shores of Llyn Ogwen, my eyes were drawn up to the intimidating crest of Tryfan. I watched as climbers grappled with the hard rocky buttresses, while walkers with brightly coloured cagoules clambered towards the skyline. The seeds of my interest in the mountains were sown.

A couple of years later, I ventured onto the hills as a member of a school party intent on doing four days of the Pennine Way. Not even the cumbersome pack that was hoisted onto my back could subdue my high spirits as we set forth from Malham. Fifty miles later I sat on the return coach yearning for a hot bath, but content in the knowledge that I would never again have to set foot on another mountain. Why then did I say yes when the teacher, Jim Pickering, asked if I would be interested in further excursions? Was it that I actually enjoyed battling against driving rain and gale-force winds, soaked to the bone by damp impenetrable mists? Had I derived some perverse pleasure from the wet peat that slurped around my boots, inside and out?

Quite quickly I became the perfect peak-bagger. The lists at the back of my Wainwright and Poucher were sprinkled with little ticks. Eventually, I stood again at the foot of Tryfan, which was to be my first Welsh Three Thousander. All routes to the top are mercilessly steep and I forged up the north ridge with a sense of exhilaration and purpose. At the top I was rewarded with views as good as I have seen anywhere in the world. That day I covered as many miles as I possibly could, seeking out every delightful corner of Glyder Fach, Glyder Fawr and Y Garn before descending the mystical Devil's Kitchen. I was spellbound – like a child let loose in a chocolate factory.

Like many mountain men before me, I was fascinated by Thomas Firbank's account of the Welsh Three Thousands race in his book *I Bought a Mountain*. It was Firbank who laid down the basic rules that stand today: that the race starts on the top of Snowdon, finishes on Foel-fras, and that the tops of all the eligible summits must be touched on the way.

In those days it was accepted that there were fourteen summits with a drop of at least fifty feet in all directions. Since the Ordnance Survey's re-measurement, the Carneddau peak of Carnedd Uchaf has been judged to be 3038 feet above sea level and thus has been added to the list. If you adhered to the Scottish 'Munro' rules there would only be eight Welsh Three Thousands. Crib Goch, Carnedd Ugain, Glyder Fach, Pen yr Ole Wen, Yr Elen, Foel Grach and Carnedd Uchaf would all be omitted. Conversely I have heard it said that Castell y Gwynt on Glyder Fach and Clogwyn y Person on Carnedd Ugain would qualify under the fifty foot rule. Mathematics has no business in the mountains and I do not wish to get bogged down in classification of what constitutes a peak or mountain. Nobody will make me believe Crib Goch is not a true mountain.

The Three Thousands route is 27 miles long including the ascent of Snowdon and the walk-out from Foel-fras. It involves some 13,000ft of ascent – a very serious expedition, especially in less than perfect conditions, for it crosses some of the most rugged mountains in the British Isles. The inexperienced may well be intimidated by the exposed ridges and steep descents.

The terrain is diverse. Snowdon's is one of magnificent rock slabs and pyramids linked by razor-edge ridges. The Glyders are every bit as rugged – a chaos of bouldery summits and craggy, lake-filled cwms. The Carneddau's wide, grassy plateaux are a delight to walk but can be confusing when the mist hangs low. Never is the need for a compass so great as on the Carneddau.

Some may feel that the 27 miles is a task too great to be completed in one day and may wish to divide the walk into more manageable sections. Enjoyable ways to accomplish these are by youth hostelling or backpacking. The Youth Hostel Association has made many improvements over the years. They can now offer comfortable accommodation and a chance to socialise with people with similar interests. The hostels are listed in the data section at the back of the book. Backpacking offers a great flexibility of schedule – you can stop and pitch when you have had enough, for there are many wonderful high-level wild campsites on all three mountain ranges in addition to the conveniently placed official valley sites. It must be stressed however that the route is only suitable for experienced backpackers. Steep descents and loose screes are more dangerous with the encumbrance of a heavy rucksack.

I felt that it would be a good idea to include sections on the Snowdon Horseshoe and also the Welsh One Thousand Metre Peaks Race. Both are classic routes in their own right and offer a different perspective on the mountains of the region.

Ronald Turnbull gets up his hills somewhat faster than I do. He's not content with just fifteen peaks, but will show you how to do the forty-seven of them in the Paddy Buckley Round and even more in the Dragon's Back, a race devised by Ian Waddell and loosely based on the Snowdonia to Gower route.

It has been almost twenty years since that first memorable journey over the Pennines and, in that time, I have never lost my feeling for mountain country. I am still spellbound by Wales; I am still drawn to its mountains. I have tramped the same ground many times, but no two walks have ever been the same; the sun's rays, shadows cast by clouds, secretive mists and gleaming snows have each interpreted in their own way the timeless mountainscapes.

Roy Clayton: Blackpool December 1996

Introduction to the third edition

In the dark days of 1940 wartime Britain found its imagination captured by the account of an Englishman turned Welsh sheep farmer. Embedded in the agricultural matter of *I Bought a Mountain,* like grit in an old sock, is the achievement of a record about which very few had even heard: the fourteen three thousand foot peaks of Wales, in a time of under nine hours. In the late sixties I was just learning what 3000ft of ascent actually means in terms of exhaustion, peppermint sweeties and total separation from the world below. I read with fascinated incomprehension the exploits of Joss Naylor. He covered nearly eleven thousand feet over fourteen Welsh mountains in four and three quarter hours: that's how long it took the teenage me to climb just one Munro.

Twenty years later, I discovered for myself the pains and pleasures of fell running. Incomprehension shrank, while so did the times: mine across the hills of Scotland and those across the Welsh Threes, with Colin Donnelly recording a mere 4 hrs 20 mins in 1988.

For the ordinary but ambitious hillwalker the Welsh 3000s route is a once-in-a-lifetime 24-hour challenge. Among such ultimate walks (the Lakes 3000s, the Lyke Wake Walk, the Yorkshire Three Peaks) we think that the Welsh 3000s is the finest. The ordinary fellrunner, in pursuit of his own eccentric excellence, submits to hours of training under winter streetlights, years of twisted ankles, knee-damage and even a horrible mauve and orange club vest. The reward for all this is that the likes of the Welsh 3000s becomes a simple day trip; a substantial day trip, certainly, but still one of perhaps a half dozen such outings in a summer. Well, until that knee injury comes back.

Such runners may be aiming for a fast time, whether that's Thomas Firbank's 8 1/2 hours, or 6 hours, or even Colin Donnelly's 4 hours 20 minutes. These will take a conventional 'downhill' direction, and study carefully Route Variation S2, which saves nearly two minutes on the descent from Crib Goch. Others may run it purely for pleasure. They might take it southbound, knowing their extra speed would let them take

in the scrambling ascents of Tryfan and of Glyder Fawr's Bristly Ridge, and still get to Snowdon in time for the last train down.

For runners, the once-in-a-lifetime 24-hour challenge is the round of 47 tops devised by Paddy Buckley.

Starting from Llanberis, Buckley's Round traverses the Glyderau and the southern Carneddau before climbing Moel Siabod from Plas y Brenin. It continues over the Moelwyns to Cnicht, then crosses to the range west of Snowdon known as the Eifionydd (or as the Nantlle ridge). Finally, it makes a long high crossing of the Snowdon group to finish over Moel Eilio. It's an even better route than the well-known Bob Graham Round of the English Lake District, for at seven different points it runs along the high sharp ridges. These, whether of grass or rock, are the best of running or of walking.

On the Crib y Ddysgl ridge of Carnedd Uchaf, heading for Yr Wyddfa. Behind, the snow-covered comb of Crib Goch. Back left, the Glyderau; back right, Moel Siabod

The Paddy Buckley Round is also even longer than the Bob Graham Round. At 62 miles, with 29,000ft of ascent and no relaxing road sections, it turns out to be that annoying little bit more than ordinary runners can manage in the time. But, as it's such fun, why not linger over it? Pack up a little lightweight tent and take it over four days (which is still pretty vigorous), or a week (for those who take their lingering seriously). At whatever speed, it's an intensive experience of high Snowdonia and a truly over-the-top backpack expedition.

Over even more tops was the Dragon's Back of 1992. For a taste of the full splendour and absurdity of fell running I add a brief account of this, the longest ever run over the British hills. Over five days, two hundred miles and 45,000ft of ascent, it stretched the concept of going up Snowdon to the limit and well beyond. But the longest ever walk up Snowdon was Ann Bowker's one that started at Neath and on the way crossed every single one of Wales' 2000ft summits.

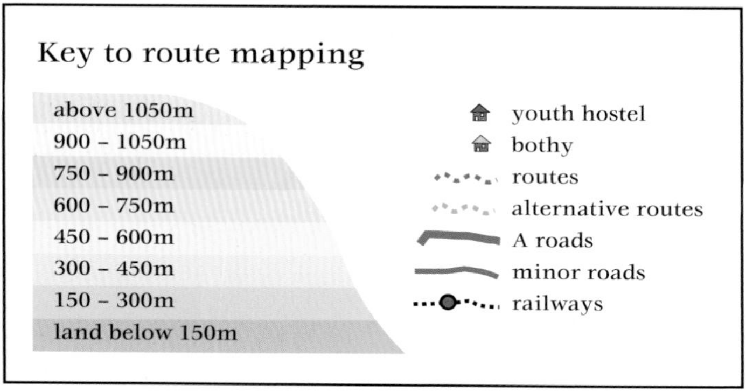

It's now 12 years since the first edition, and nine years even since the second edition, the one with Joss Naylor on the cover. Advances in colour printing mean that we can now offer a book that's entirely in colour, while still keeping to the 'pretty inexpensive' ethos of hill-runners and my sort of hill walkers. Alas, the colour printing makes even more evident the mid-range price-tag and well-worn condition of my mountain gear...

In ten years, paths grow, shift across the scree, and get rebuilt by the National Park path people. Stiles become gates, forests get felled, and a new narrow-gauge railway runs around the base of Snowdon. For this new version of the book, the routes have all been revisited, and updated where necessary.

The passing of ten years brings other changes as well. I'm less interested than I was in doing the Welsh 3000s very very quickly: instead, I aim to do them in the most amusing way I can invent. This might be considered as an attack of late-onset maturity. It means that my 2003 crossing of the Welsh 3000s took slightly over 24 hours, from the bothy at Dulyn by way of Tryfan's north ridge and the Glyders' Bristly one, to a bivvy on Snowdon summit, for a dawn finale over Y Lliwedd. As before, we detail the standard northbound route for both standard walkers and record-breaking runners. But this new edition gives more prominence to the southbound (Foel-fras first) route, with those classic scrambles on Tryfan and Glyder Fach included, for any who don't think fifteen Welsh summits on their own are enough fun for a single day out.

To make space for that, while still keeping the book back-pocket sized, we've greatly abridged the Dragon's Back Race, from Conwy to the Black Mountain. Well, 1992 is now, sadly, rather a long time ago. Before the last second-hand copies of the old edition finally become illegible under Snowdonian rain and peat-stains, you can search the Internet for 'Welsh Three Thousand Foot Challenges' ISBN 0 9515996 6 6.

Ronald Turnbull Dumfriesshire March 2010

How to use this book

The sketch-mapping in this book is not intended for navigation on the hill. A properly surveyed and full-sized map is required for that. The relevant ones are listed in Section 10.

Where we write 'path', the path is one too narrow for any wheeled vehicle, even a quad bike. A footway that's wide enough for a rugged vehicle is referred to as 'track'. The exceptions are the "Pig Track" and the "Miners' Track" as those are their traditional names. (Actually, parts of them are wide enough for cars.) A measurement such as 100m is a vertical height. 100 metres, with 'etres', represents a horizontal or sloping distance. We use the name 'Snowdon' for the complex mountain with its many tops: the Welsh 'Yr Wyddfa' for the main summit. So that Yr Wyddfa, Crib Goch, Y Lliwedd etc are all summits of 'Snowdon'.

The timings for routes up Snowdon, and elsewhere, are based on a formula where 120m of ascent counts as 1km of extra distance, and then reckoning 4.5km per hour. Extra is added for particularly rough ground and scrambling. That is a moderate pace for a moderate walker. For the Welsh 3000s, we've assumed you're an immoderate walker and a bit quicker than that.

Mountain walking is not without risk, and in winter or over rocky ground and scrambling, even more so. This book does not instruct in the hill skills required for covering the wonderful Welsh mountain ground it describes. Readers must satisfy themselves that they are suitably experienced and equipped for these challenging and arduous walks.

1

Ten Ways to the Top of Snowdon

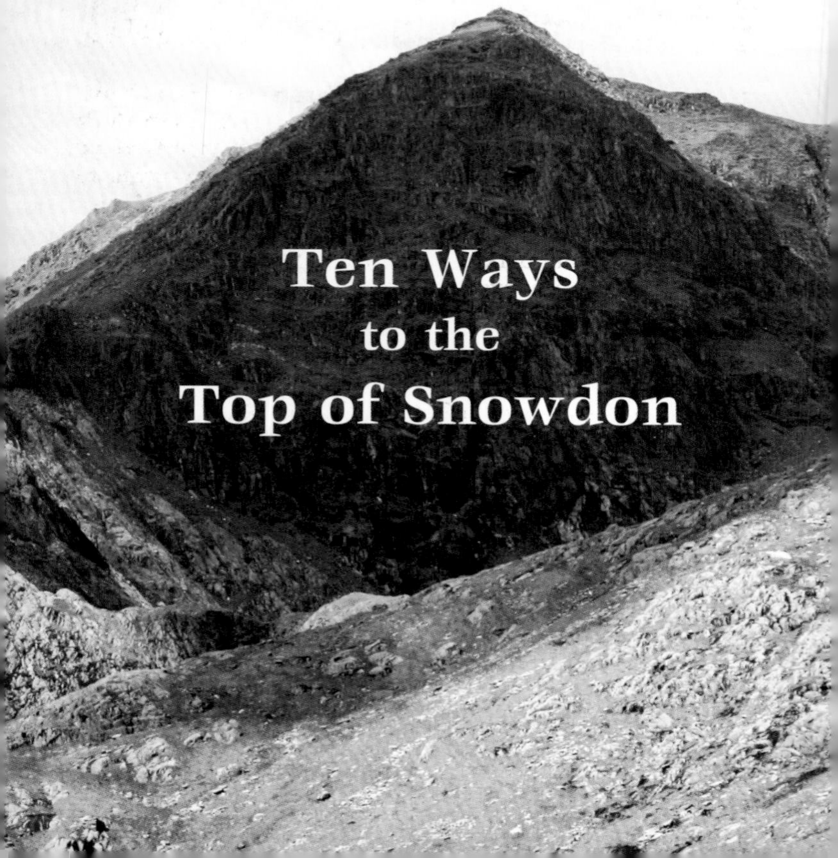

There are ten main ways up Snowdon, and not one of them is a bad one. One of them, of course, is the Crib Goch Pinnacles, which takes ordinary walkers onto higher and scarier scrambling than anywhere else they're ever likely to want to do. 600m below, and altogether different in atmosphere, there's the dark gloomy hole of Llyn Llydaw, with dripping dark crags rising into dripping dark clouds, and you go over the lip to find an even deeper, even gloomier and more dripping hole containing Glaslyn.

Another favourite is the one from Nantgwynant, the one that isn't the Watkin Path but heads into the col behind Yr Aran, to reach Yr Wyddfa by its sharp southern ridge. I've only ever done that one in mist and rain, and the rain flies sideways through the little rocky gaps, and the mist swirls in vertical circles behind the pinnacles, and it's all very satisfying.

But then, so are the other seven ways. Very satisfying is the under-appreciated and steep little scramble of Y Gribin. Very satisfying is the Ranger Path, on a day when the smooth grass is hot to lie on, and sunlight twinkles in the tarns in the bottoms of the chasms on either hand, and there's time to linger and stretch out that western ridge all the way to Moel Eilio.

Left: Yr Wyddfa from the Miners Track
Above: Snowdon summit, as it appeared before its 2008 refit, on a typically busy summer day

Ten top routes – by wide ridges, and narrow ridges, and the dark hollow of Glaslyn (not to mention the railway). And even then, Snowdon's richness is far from being exhausted. For the long ascent by way of Y Lliwedd, see Chapter 4 (Snowdon Horseshoe). For an untrodden, romantic, and steep way from Nant Peris, see Chapter 5 (Welsh 3000s North to South).

Two routes, the Pig Track and the Llanberis Path, are described also in descent.

Routes to the top of Snowdon

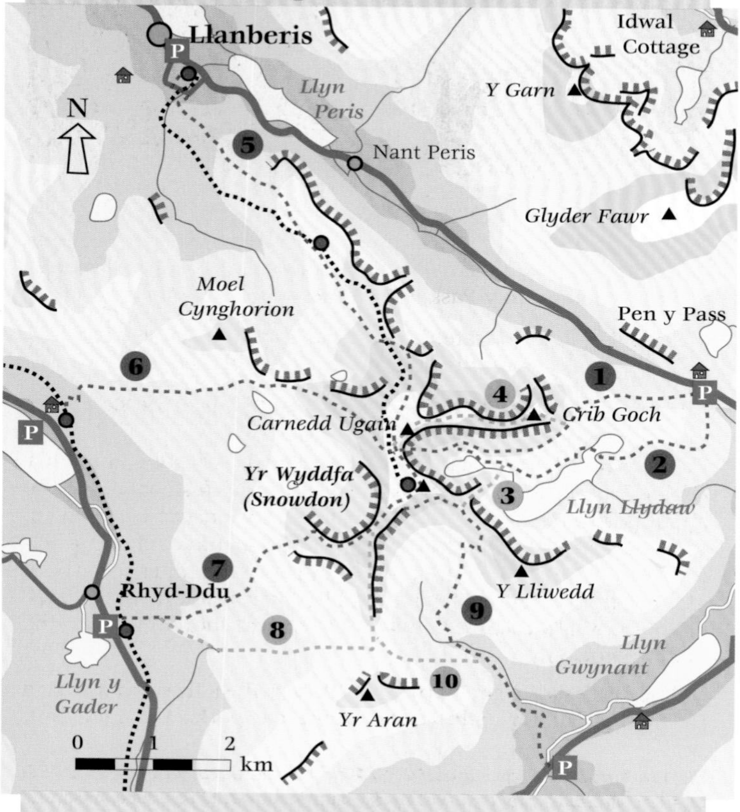

ROUTE 1	The Pig Track
Distance	5km (3 miles)
Ascent	750m
Start	Pen y Pass, SH647556
Difficulty	Moderate. The Zigzags can hold snow even when the rest of the mountain is clear.
Time	2 hr 30 min – 3 hr up; up to 2 hr in descent

This is sometimes referred to as the Pyg Track after the Pen y Gwryd Hotel (though it starts at Pen y Pass and so would be the Pyp Track, no?) The route actually takes its name from Bwlch y Moch (Pass of the Pigs). It's the most scenic of the popular routes up Snowdon and one of the quicker ones for those attempting the 3000s. The path is also easy to follow in the dark (in the uphill direction, anyway) if you are intending bivvying out on Snowdon.

The Pig Track begins from the **Pen y Pass** through a gap in the wall at the top right corner of the car park. A flagged path

Pig Track below the zig-zags, with Yr Wyddfa's northeast face above. In full winter conditions, the final part of the path ices up and can become severe. (Photo: James Clayton)

blasts its way through rocky outcrops above the Pass of Llanberis with the imposing peak of Crib Goch dominating views ahead. Several years ago this path underwent significant repair work and the result was somewhat akin to a motorway. The passage of millions of boots has moulded the route into a pleasing track with good views of the Llanberis Pass.

After climbing the chunky rock steps for half an hour or so, the path veers left to **Bwlch y Moch** (569m), where spectacular views of Cwm Dyli appear with the cliffs of Lliwedd soaring from Llyn Llydaw. A wooden marker post points the way to the left over a double ladder stile. (The path to the right is sign-posted 'Crib Goch' and marks the start of the Snowdon Horseshoe.)

Our route now skirts the lower southern slopes of Crib Goch running parallel to the Miners' Track a couple of hundred feet below us. The path gradually climbs to a second higher cwm. Here the blue-green waters of Glaslyn lie cradled in the arms of Yr Wyddfa, Carnedd Ugain and the rocky spur of Y Gribin. The path drops over a grassy bluff and continues past a stone marker. This is where the Miners' Track rises to greet us.

The path continues across a loose, worn area of rock to reach the infamous zigzags, a robustly constructed stairway that climbs towards Bwlch Glas, the pass between Yr Wyddfa and Carnedd Ugain. Marker posts have been erected in the last year or so in the latter stages. The path levels out before reaching the obelisk at **Bwlch Glas**.

Turn left, tracing the cliff's edge parallel to the line of the Snowdon Railway to the summit. Sometimes people follow the course of the railway to the summit but this can be dangerous and is unnecessary as the path hereabouts has now been improved.

Descent: take the broad path just above the railway to **Bwlch Glas**, where a stone pillar marks the top of the Pig Track. Turn right, steeply downhill, on rough stony zigzags. (Old snow can lie late on this slope. If necessary, divert onto the Llanberis path. Even if you miss the last Sherpa bus, there's a good chance of hitching a lift from Llanberis up to Pen y Pass.)

In the dark, take care when descending the zig-zags below Bwlch Glas. It's possible to miss a doubling-back of the path and keep going straight ahead out into the stones and small crags below Crib y Ddysgl.

At 750m (SH 6144 5482) is the path junction where the Pig Track slants gently around the hill slope eastwards, while the Miners Track continues steeply downwards to Glaslyn. (It really doesn't matter if you do take the Miners Track by mistake.) The Pig Track contours above Llyn Llydaw to pass through **Bwlch y Moch** (SH 6332 5525). Now wide and rebuilt, it heads down northeast at first then bends eastwards, descending only gently. At last the lights of the youth hostel glow ghostly through the mist.

ROUTE 2	The Miners Track
Distance	6km (3 3/4 miles)
Ascent	750m
Start	Pen y Pass, SH647556
Difficulty	Moderate. Very easy to Glaslyn, then steep pull to the summit. The Zigzags can hold snow even when the rest of the mountain is clear.
Time	2 hr 30 min – 3 hr up; up to 2 hr in descent

This route uses part of an old copper miners' route connecting Bethesda with the Glaslyn Mine at the foot of Yr Wyddfa. Like the Pig Track it is very scenic, offering fine views of Cwm Dyli and its cliffs.

The wide, stony path leaves the left hand side of the Pen y Pass car park. The level path contours with steep ground above on the right; if you're climbing with the uphill side on the left, you're on the Pig Track instead! The path passes **Llyn Teyrn** into Cwm Dyli. This vast hollow is filled by the expansive waters of **Llyn Llydaw**. The Gorphwysfa Club every 1st January organises a race right around the lake from Pen y Pass. Winning times are around 45 minutes, depending on snow conditions.

The lake is crossed by way of its causeway and the stony track continues along its northern shores, passing a derelict crushing mill. Soon after this the path leaves the lake shore and

Y Lliwedd from Llyn Llydaw

climbs steadily to the shores of **Glaslyn**, a small tarn tightly enclosed by the mighty slopes of Yr Wyddfa and Carnedd Ugain and cradled by the rocky spur of Y Gribin. At the termination of the old track, beyond the ruins of the old mine barracks, a stone marker post signals the end of playtime as the path turns steeply uphill towards the Pig Track. The cairned path struggles over loose, stony slopes to join the **Pig Track**. The combined path zigzags to the obelisk at **Bwlch Glas**.

From here a left turn takes you alongside the railway to the summit.

ROUTE 3	scramble up Y Gribin
Distance	6km (3 3/4 miles)
Ascent	750m
Start	Pen y Pass, SH647556
Difficulty	Grade 1 scramble, quite steep and exposed
Time	2 hr 30 min – 3 hr

The Gribin is a slightly more serious scramble than Crib Goch, just as good, and much, much quieter. Combine the two for a great Snowdon circuit.

From **Pen y Pass** the Miners Track (Route 2) leads to the outflow of **Glaslyn**.

Turn left off the path to cross the outflow. The path bypasses on the right the first rise of the gentle ridge ahead. Better to take this rise direct on very gentle slabs and walk its flat level top with lakes below on both sides.

The path rejoins from the right, with **Y Gribin's** steepening rock spur ahead. Some trodden-on scree suggests a line to right of the rocks – ignore that. The first slabby rise is taken most easily by grooves on the right. The next, slightly steeper, 100m can be taken direct, on paths and short scrambles. The rib now gets slightly steeper, with a ledge to the left for 10 metres leading to a steep step back up to the right. 20m above, a groove slants up to the left and then back to the right.

The rest of the route is easier. Blocky scrambling and walking lead to a final steepening, taken up the crest.

A couple of cairns (useful if descending this route) mark the way straight up to the ridge crest at **Bwlch y Saethau**. Drop to the Watkin Path ahead and just below (Route 9), or turn up right for scrambly outcrops among scree (see Snowdon Horseshoe, Chapter 2).

The Gribin Ridge, heading to the base of the steep final section

ROUTE 4	Crib Goch Pinnacles
Distance	5km (3 miles)
Ascent	750m
Start	Pen y Pass, SH647556
Difficulty	Grade 1 scrambling, easy within the grade, but exposed, and serious in windy or snowy conditions.
Time	3 hr – 3 hr 30 min unless delayed by crowds

With about a mile of scrambling ground, and its magnificent ridgeline situation, this is one of the UK's classic scrambles. It can get very crowded.

For the route, see the Snowdon Horseshoe (anticlockwise) in Chapter 2. For the **descent**, see Snowdon Horseshoe (clockwise) in the same chapter.

ROUTE 5	Llanberis Path
Distance	8km (5 miles)
Ascent	980 m
Start	Llanberis SH583597
Difficulty	Easy but long. Can be awkward in winter
Time	3 hr 30 min up; 2 hr – 2 hr 30 min down

The Llanberis path is the easiest and most popular ascent of Snowdon, apart from buying a train ticket. Recent repairs have greatly improved the path up to Clogwyn Station.

At the southeast edge of the village, it leaves the main A4086 on a tarmac lane opposite the Royal Victoria Hotel. The lane climbs steeply past Penceunant Isaf Tea Rooms. Five minutes later a signpost on the left indicates the footpath to Snowdon. The Snowdon Mountain Railway is never far away and provides a little interest on a relatively dull climb on the spur rising above Afon Arddu. Halfway House (SH599569) now once again provides refreshment. Beyond Clogwyn Station the path cuts up under the railway, revealing superb lofty views of the Pass of Llanberis at Cwm Hetiau. The name means 'Valley of the Hats' because many a Victorian gentlemen lost his topper at this point. This was never too much of a problem unless your head was still in it at the time. The cwm below is presumably now full of baseball caps.

The route steepens as it veers southwards, traversing the shoulder of Carnedd Ugain past the 'Pigtop Pillar' monolith at **Bwlch Glas**, where there are exquisite views down Cwm Dyli, and finally to the summit.

Descent: This descent is on a wide and easy path. Unless under snow, the only difficulty (in the dark even) is being on the right path when leaving the Pigtop Pillar.

Head down the path above and to right of the railway to the Pigtop Pillar at Bwlch Moch. Keep on the wide path ahead, contouring, remaining *above* the railway – don't cross it. The path turns gently down left, then descends more steeply to join the railway and pass under it.

Don't keep your eyes on the path as there are fine views back to Cloggy (Clogwyn Du'r Arddu) and across to Moel Cynghorion. Soon the descent becomes gentler. You pass the **Halfway House** cafe, then turn back under the railway by another bridge. At the start of enclosed ground is a ladder stile, with a last view of Snowdon. The path leads down to a tarred lane, which descends steeply to the edge of Llanberis near the station of the Mountain Railway.

Descending the Llechog ridge on the Rhyd-ddu Path

ROUTE 6	The Snowdon Ranger Path
Distance	6km (3 1/2 miles)
Ascent	930m
Start	Snowdon Ranger Youth Hostel, Betwys Garmon SH565551
Difficulty	moderate
Time	about 3 hr

This is probably the least used of the Snowdon routes and, although not the most spectacular, it does have its moments. It is probably the safest route in the winter months.

Zigzagging across rough, grassy slopes the path gives fine views towards Moel Hebog and the Nantlle Ridge, which lie invitingly across the sparkling waters of Llyn y Gader.

As the path gains height the scene becomes more dramatic with Llyn Ffynnon-y-gwas nestling in the sullen, crag-ringed bowl of Cwm Clogwyn. Here it passes below **Bwlch Cwm Brwynog**, and now the going gets harder as it snakes up the rocky arm above Clogwyn Du'r Arddu.

Where the gradients ease, bear left to gain views of the cliffs of Clogwyn Du'r Arddu, a favoured spot for experienced climbers. It's now a simple ascent over the stony shoulder of **Carnedd Ugain** to reach the mountain railway. Cross the railway to **Bwlch Glas**, where a monolith marks the spot. Here the path turns right and follows the crest of the ridge to the left (east) of the railway to Snowdon's summit.

ROUTE 7	The Rhyd-ddu Path
Distance	6km (4 miles)
Ascent	900m
Start	Rhyd-ddu Car Park (with toilets) SH 571526
Difficulty	quite easy
Time	about 3 hr

This interesting, if unspectacular, route begins on a quarry road to the north of the large car park. It crosses the railway just to left of the station. In 200 metres take the right fork, signed for Snowdon, and 1km (3/4 mile) from the start, at SH583525, abandon the rough track (it's **Route 8**, heading for Bwlch Cwm y Llan between Yr Wyddfa and Yr Aran). A path to the left, beyond a stile, now wends its way amongst rocky outcrops to attain the **Llechog** ridge, where dark cliffs plummet in a spectacular scene to Cwm Clogwyn.

A gravelly path winds steeply uphill to **Bwlch Main** where you overlook the gigantic hollow of Cwm Tregalan towards the stony western flanks of Y Lliwedd. From Bwlch Main the path climbs steadily on a rocky ridge north-northeast (or you can scramble the true crest on the right.) Edge along to right of the new station and cafe en route to **Y Wyddfa** summit.

Descent: from Snowdon summit, start by passing to left of the new summit building to find the top of the descent ridge. Once past the pillar marking the top of the Watkin Path, the descent path is clear, though remember that there's a fork right as the ridge levels at 750m, **Bwlch Main**.

ROUTE 8	Yr Wyddfa's south ridge
Distance	6km (4 miles)
Ascent	900m
Start	Rhyd-ddu Car Park (with toilets) SH 571526
Difficulty	quite easy
Time	about 3 hr

At busy times, this is a quieter alternative to Route 7, the Rhyd-ddu path. Start as Route 7 from **Rhyd-ddu**. After 1km (3/4 mile) where that path turns off left (SH583525), continue along the quarry track to **Bwlch Cwm Llan**. Turn up left, northwards, on Yr Wyddfa's southern ridge, to rejoin the Rhyd-ddu route at **Bwlch Main**.

Descent: from Snowdon summit, start by passing to left of the new summit building to find the top of the descent ridge. Once past the pillar marking the top of the Watkin Path, the descent path is clear. As the ridge levels at 750m, **Bwlch Main**, fork up left on the main ridge path. At 550m, just above **Bwlch Cwm Llan**, the built path bears down left for Nant Gwynant but here fork off right to follow the broken wall down to a cairn in the col. Here the right-of-way for Rhyd-ddu turns off right.

ROUTE 9	The Watkin Path
Distance	6.5km (4 miles)
Ascent	1050m
Start	Lay-by car park, Pont Bethania, SH 628506
Difficulty	More ascent and tougher than other routes
Time	3hr – 3 hr 30 min up; about 2 hr down

The path takes its name from Sir Edward Watkin, a wealthy railway owner who engineered it as a donkey track. It was opened by Prime Minister William Gladstone in 1892. The path gained further fame as a stunt double for the Khyber Pass in the 'Carry On' film.

Right: Watkin Path below Bwlch y Saethau, with Yr Wyddfa summit above. The direct line to the summit involves some scrambling: the path diverts over screes to the left.
Below: the pillar at the top of the Watkin Path (photos: James Clayton)

Cross Afon Glaslyn into the tarmac lane opposite the lay-by, but at once take a new path up ahead, signed 'Watkin Path'. This runs through woods just above the lane, crosses a wooden footbridge, and rejoins the lane's continuation track in the beautiful glen of the Afon Cwm Llan. After passing some impressive waterfalls, the path climbs into **Cwm Llan** dominated by the huge precipices of Craig-ddu, with the Snowdon massif forming the background. Cross the stream by the ruins of Plascwmllan, once a quarry manager's house.

On reaching Gladstone Rock, the route veers westwards to circumvent Craig-ddu. It then climbs to the barren **Cwm Tregalan**, which is hemmed in by the ramparts of Yr Wyddfa and Y Lliwedd. After passing the ruined barracks and spoil heaps of another slate quarry, the Watkin Path heads north-east out of the cwm. In the upper reaches it zigzags over the stony wilderness of Lliwedd's western flanks to attain **Bwlch Ciliau**, overlooking Cwm Dyli and its huge lake, Llyn Llydaw. There are wonderful views of Yr Wyddfa (L) together with the bold dark cliffs of Y Lliwedd (R).

You have now joined the Snowdon Horseshoe route. A wide path aims north-west for Bwlch y Saethau, a short way down to left of the crest of the fairly level, airy ridge.

Beyond **Bwlch y Saethau**, the ascent to Yr Wyddfa's summit is steep and care should be exercised. Small paths will be seen heading straight up the edge ahead, but that route is loose and awkward except for scramblers – see Snowdon Horseshoe page 35. The less uncomfortable way contours out left, to rake up the steep scree slope above Cwm Tregalan. The path is rather loose underfoot, but wide and clear. It reaches Snowdon's South Ridge at a stone obelisk (SH608542). Turn up right, to the summit.

Descent: as on the previous route, from Snowdon summit, start by passing to left of the new summit building to find the top of the descent ridge. After 300 metres, and possibly a few metres left of the path you're on, the pillar marks the turnoff left across the scree slope at the head of **Cwm Tregalan**.

ROUTE 10	Bwlch Cwm Llan and the South Ridge
Distance	6.5km (4 miles)
Ascent	1050m
Start	Lay-by car park, Pont Bethania, SH 628506
Difficulty	Tough, but slightly gentler than the Watkin Path
Time	3hr – 3 hr 30 min up; about 2 hr down

Less crowded than the Watkin Path, this variant also avoids the treacherous screes on the final pull to the summit. There is still much ascent and it's quite arduous.

Turn left off the Watkin Path at SH622520, just before it crosses the river, and climb to the old quarry tramway. Turn right along this for 250 metres, until a path turns up left (SH617521). The path climbs towards **Bwlch Cwm Llan**, the pass between Yr Wyddfa and Yr Aran. Just before reaching the col the path angles right to climb onto Yr Wyddfa's pleasant south ridge, which is then followed as on Route 8, to the summit.

last steps up Snowdon's north ridge to the summit

2

The Snowdon Horseshoe

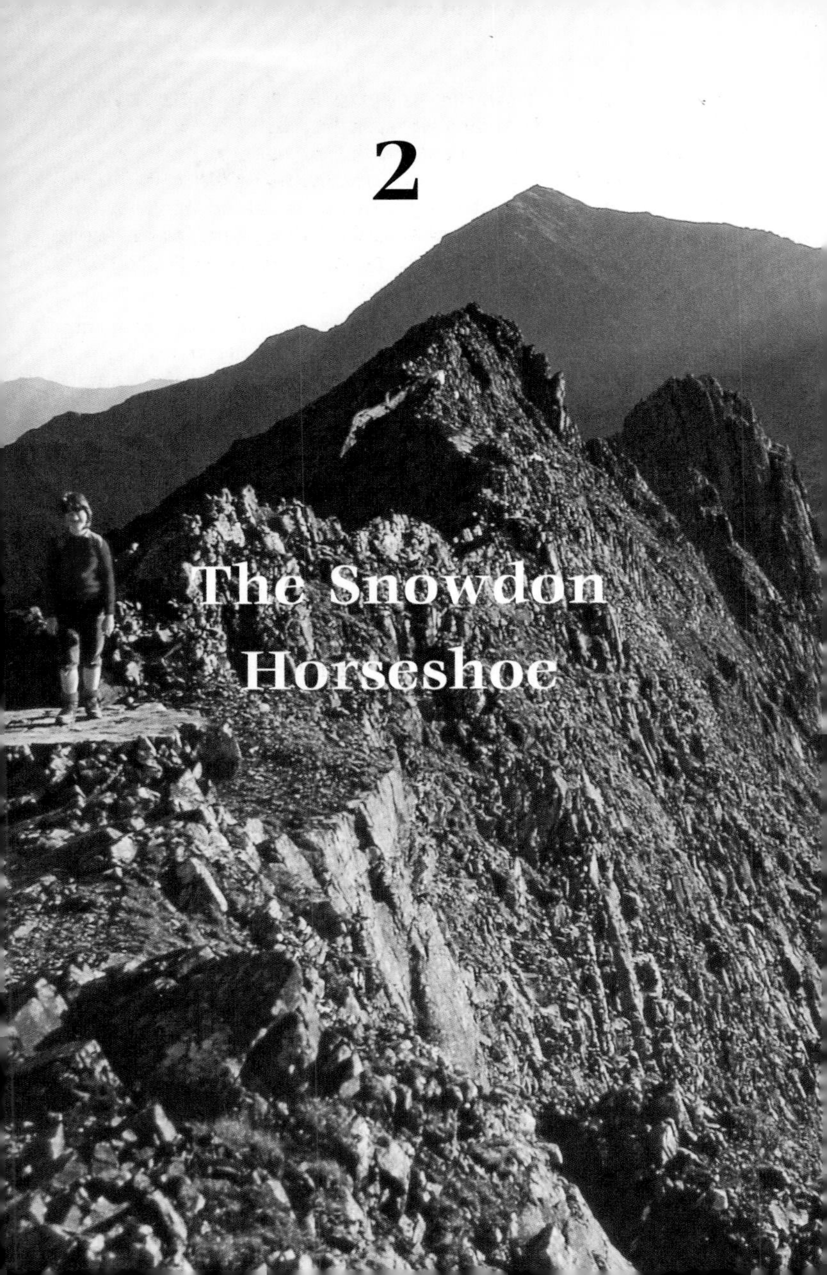

Previous page: on Crib Goch's north summit, with the main summit and the Crib Goch pinnacles behind, and Yr Wyddfa summit above (Photo: Phil Iddon)

THE SNOWDON HORSESHOE	
Distance	11km (7 miles)
Ascent	1000m
Start/finish	Pen y Pass, SH647556
Difficulty	includes Grade 1 scrambling in fairly exposed situations
Time	5 hr - 6 hr

The Snowdon Horseshoe is one of the finest ridge walks in Europe. It takes the description 'ridge' to the limit, for paths in some places become non-existent as the foot-moulded razor-edged crests tumble into the valleys, leaving the walker exposed and occasionally uneasy.

In wintry conditions, the Horseshoe is a very serious mountaineering exercise and, sadly, claims many lives. It should only be attempted by those equipped with and proficient in the use of both crampons and an ice axe.

Most people start the walk from Pen y Pass youth hostel and make for Crib Goch on the Pig Track, and we describe this below, but I think that to do it in the reverse order is even better. Firstly, the loose upper sections of the Watkin Path are much easier when crossed uphill; and secondly, I think the prospects from the Crib Goch to Crib y Ddysgl Ridge are more interesting when seen from this direction. Also there will be fewer people on the first section over Y Lliwedd if you have an early start.

Take the broad Miners Track from the left hand side of **Pen y Pass** car park, heading in a southerly direction. A good pace can be maintained over the path, which gains little height at first.

The path continues past derelict copper-mining cottages overlooking **Llyn Teyrn**, a small tarn set in a secret grassy hollow among small bluffs. The lake is home to brown trout

Snowdon Horseshoe

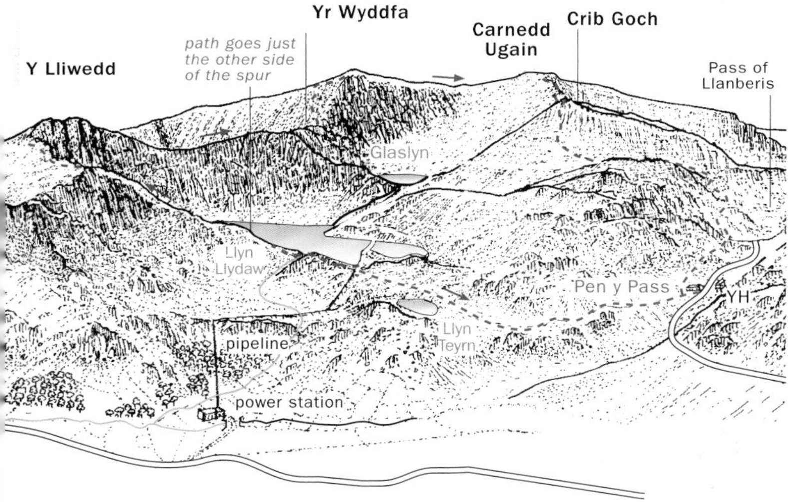

if you have forgotten your butties. The path climbs out of the hollow to a poorly camouflaged pale green corrugated iron shed on the shores of **Llyn Llydaw**, the much larger lake that occupies the vast chasm of Cwm Dyli.

Here we leave the crowds on the old Miners Track (which blazes a course up Cwm Dyli) and head south on a flag-stoned path. Cross a footbridge, and after a slight dip through boggy flat ground, the collar work commences on an arduous ascent towards Y Lliwedd. The stony track gains height rapidly as it weaves around a series of rock ledges to attain the ridge by a large cairn (SH631535) to the northeast of Lliwedd Bach. Although the

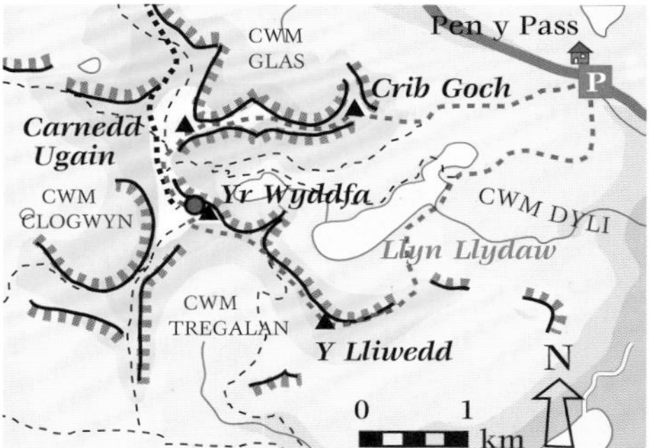

majesty of Snowdon and its satellites dominates, it is pleasing to see the contrasting softer scenery contained in the wide sweep of Nant Gwynant to the south. Its shimmering lakes and lush pastures are patched with woodland and fringed with the gritty knolls of the Moelwyn–Siabod ridge.

The route now continues along the cliff edge to **Lliwedd Bach**. This will be remembered for its secret niches offering views of the dark precipices of both East and West Lliwedd, which tower three hundred metres above Llyn Llydaw. The bouldery cairned path keeps close to the edge before clambering over both the **Lliwedd** summits.

The path now descends on heavily bouldered slopes to the northwest. Take care not to venture too far right on the descent here as you may find yourself crag bound. At **Bwlch Ciliau** it's joined by the popular Watkin Path to Yr Wyddfa's summit. Continue along the ridge to **Bwlch y Saethau** (Pass of the Arrows) where Wyddfa's pyramid casts its shadow. There is a wonderful retrospective view down the length of Cwm Dyli, taking in Crib y Ddysgl, Crib Goch and the latter part of the Horseshoe.

There is a confusing network of paths at the pass, including one that descends the spur of Y Gribin and some that just visit the edge above Glaslyn. In mist it is best to stick to the main route, which here contours below and left of the crest of the ridge, overlooking the vast hollow of Cwm Tregalan.

The final stages of the route to Snowdon's summit can be tricky for its flanks are steep and the shaly surface rock is friable. Two paths exist. The one to the right aims for the summit directly, a scramble that some but not all enjoy: it is described just below. The more comfortable route slants left across the slippery southern slopes. It climbs steeply for the final 200m up the south face of Snowdon, twisting and turning to reach Snowdon's south ridge at a rock monolith. Here the Watkin Path and the Rhyd-ddu Path meet for a joint onslaught on the summit a mere 10 minutes away. Looking westwards, the impressive peaks of the Nantlle Ridge and Mynydd Mawr form the backdrop to Rhyd-ddu and the nearby lakes of Cwellyn, Gader and Dywarchan.

Looking across the Snowdon Horseshoe from Glyder Fawr. The steep path onto Y Lliwedd is seen on the left. Y Lliwedd's skyline runs down right, to Bwlch y Saethau. In the foreground, Crib Goch's east ridge runs down to Bwlch y Moch.

It's now just a short, easy climb to **Yr Wyddfa** summit, passing to the right of the new café en route. The summit cairn is usually swarming with tourists, many of whom have made the journey on the Mountain Railway. They will share with you one of the great panoramas of Europe. Although not of alpine proportions, the view from Yr Wyddfa reveals magnificent glacial architecture in a labyrinth of cwms, aretes and buttresses. In good conditions half of Wales can be seen, its coastline, distant towns and range upon range of mountains, paling to the horizon.

Direct route from Bwlch y Saethau to Yr Wyddfa: the steep spur has low outcrops emerging from unpleasant loose scree lying over rock. Small paths lead up to the base of the scree. By seeking out the scrambling on the rock outcrops, a pleasant ascent can be made. At 1000m altitude the spur becomes abruptly less steep. A small path zig-zags up scree to Yr Wyddfa summit.

The first (westernmost) of Crib Goch's pinnacles. Behind, Glaslyn and the Gribin Ridge. Two walkers rest on the more exposed route on the pinnacle's northern flank. The easier route bypasses the pinnacle on the Glaslyn flank, then arrives up the rocky gully from down left.

From **Yr Wyddfa**, descend north-northwest, on the wide path. Just below is the railway, with the sudden brink of Cwm Dyli just above on your right. The heavily rebuilt path runs down to **Bwlch Glas**, the pass between Yr Wyddfa and Carnedd Ugain. The spot is marked by the 'Pigtop Pillar', a huge obelisk where walkers using both the Miners and Pig Track gain the ridge.

Beyond the obelisk, a sprawling cairn marks the departure of the popular Llanberis path. Our route veers up slightly to the right, still keeping to the edge of Cwm Dyli. The wide, cairned path affords an easy pace as it climbs to **Carnedd Ugain's** flaking white trig point.

On the way down Carnedd Ugain you are confronted by a choice of well-worn paths. This can be confusing in mist. It is advisable to maintain an easterly direction, close to the edge of Cwm Dyli, as this is where the path materialises when the ridge narrows. After dropping into a hollow there is a magnificent view back to Yr Wyddfa. The crest of the ridge is now followed before veering a few feet to the left of a rocky buttress. In favourable conditions the arete itself is the finest course as the climber is challenged to clamber over a kilometre of rocky bluffs and clefts. The use of hands and occasionally bottoms will be needed here. The course ceases to be obvious as the ridge appears to terminate abruptly at a cliff face. A path is available to the right however, descending steeply some 15m by a series of ledges. The ridge continues rocky to the broad grassy pass, **Bwlch Goch** 858m (marked Coch on current maps).

The first of the **Crib Goch Pinnacles** now lies ahead.

The most satisfying way is the one over the knife-edged crest, although this is very exposed and not suitable for those with a nervous disposition or on a bicycle. This higher route starts its ascent on the right hand side of the first pinnacle, where a steep path quickly attains the top. Shuffle along a narrow shelf before dropping down the left side to the depression.
The easier way contours around this first pinnacle on its right (Llyn Llydaw) side. Head up the pinnacle about half way, where it steepens. Now a rock ledge contours round to the right, taking you across the rock face to the stony gully behind the pinnacle. Head left, up this, to its top.

The second pinnacle is tackled from the right side. Continue along the ridge for about 200 metres to a pile of stones marking **Crib Goch's** true summit (923m at SH624551).

The next stage is the narrowest of all. The good scrambling is on blocky rocks immediately below and to the right of the crest, which is used as a handrail. There is also an exposed, gravelly path a few metres further down to the right; we consider the scrambling to be not only more fun but also, with its firm rock, the safer choice.

Crib Goch's more celebrated **North Summit** (921m) is marked by a polished circular rock platform and a meeting of ridges (room for one, please book early).

The descent from Crib Goch is tricky, especially in snow and ice. It begins with an airy passage over shaly slopes eastwards towards Bwlch y Moch. The way down moderately angled blocky rocks was marked by a couple of helpful cairns when last I passed. This terrain ends abruptly as the rock steepens below. Here head down to the right, with good, well-worn holds for hand and foot.

After about 15m of rather steep downward scrambling the slope eases. Now a cairned path heads down, slightly on the right (Llyn Llydaw) flank, between scrambly outcrops. The path winds down the still steep lower slopes to meet the Pig Track at **Bwlch y Moch**.

The newly renovated track is somewhat overdone and unsympathetic to its surroundings. To be fair, several years of wear and regrowth have somewhat smoothed it into the landscape, and it does offer a quick way back to base at **Pen y Pass**. It also has good views of the harsh boulder-strewn Pass of Llanberis and the rocky crest of Esgair Felen.

SNOWDON HORSESHOE ANTICLOCKWISE

From the back right-hand corner of **Pen y Pass** car park, behind the Gorphwysfa Café, take the tarred path waymarked 'PyG Track' past a helipad. After a wall gap it becomes stones and gravel. A section slightly downhill between boulders has views ahead down Llanberis Pass. Then the path turns up left to **Bwlch y Moch** (Pig Pass).

Just beyond the crest of the pass turn right, marked 'Crib Goch'. The path crosses a ladder stile with a warning that this path goes to Crib Goch. The path slants up the left (Llyn Llydaw) flank, with occasional scrambly bits, where you can take the slightly more challenging lines as practice.

The path regains the crest for a steep rocky section. Here a well-worn set of holds up a slightly out-of-balance groove is the hardest part of the route. Above this the route heads up right, onto the right (Llanberis Pass) flank. A couple of cairns may mark the way, which heads up gently-angled blocky ground, to reach the **north summit** (921m) of **Crib Goch**.

Looking east from Yr Wyddfa to Crib Goch and Llyn Llydaw

The crest continues as blocky ground, all footholds, but exposed on the right. A path runs 10 metres down the left hand flank but it's probably safer to stay on bare rock, just below and left of the crest. At the end of this section you pass over **Crib Goch's** main (923m) summit. Contour around the first two pinnacles around their bases, to a notch before the **third pinnacle**.

Here an exposed scramblers' route passes up to right of this final pinnacle. But easier is to head down left in a gully of spiky holds for 30m height loss. Don't go too far down: the scree below the turnoff point looks walked-on but has simply slid down. Look out for a well-trodden ledge heading out right (for someone facing downhill), across the base of the pinnacle, then heading up to the crest behind. A steep path leads down bare rock to the levelling at **Bwlch Goch**.

The main path leads along the crest, then just down to its left (or there's a smaller path weaving among rocks along the crestline). After 200 metres the main path rejoins the ridge crest. Ahead, the crest is rockier and slightly steeper. Here avoid taking a contouring path left, but head straight up the crest, by easy scrambling, possibly slightly to right of the crest line.

After another levelling, a steeper tower could start with a short steep wall which has good holds – or head round left for easier lines. Continue up the left flank of the tower, on good scrambling with large holds, to the crest behind it. This crest is blocky-rocky, as Crib Goch was, but now with the easiest line a few metres down to right (Llanberis Pass side), or on a path just below.

The ridge becomes stony, with a large sprawling cairn almost filling a small col. The path continues along the crest, with some rocky obstructions avoided by the path, though they can be pleasantly scrambled over. A steeper step is climbed up by a 10m groove on the right, with the trig on **Carnedd Ugain** not far beyond.

A wide stony path leads down to the Pigtop Pillar in **Bwlch Glas** where the Pig Track arrives from down on the left. A wide path continues to left of the railway, with drops to Glaslyn and great views just up on the left, to **Yr Wyddfa** summit.

Yr Wyddfa Southeast Ridge: descent: this alternative route leads down to steep screes and outcrops, but can be enjoyed by scramblers (Grade 1 in descent).

A small path heads down from the cairn, becoming a zig-zag scree path. The ridge abruptly steepens, to a ground of outcrops and scree. The scree is nasty, but the outcrop ground gives some down-scrambling on clean well-used rock. Below the outcrops, the slope eases to the narrow ridgeline that passes through Bwlch y Saethau.

For the more comfortable route from Snowdon summit, head down southwest, finding a path passing to left of the cafe. It leads down into a pleasant ridgeline. After 200 metres, you'll see on the left the obelisk marking the Watkin Path turnoff. Here turn off left on a fairly wide path sloping gently down across a steep, loose slope. At its end the path passes along just below and to right of the ridgeline that defines **Bwlch y Saethau**.

After 500 metres, with Y Lliwedd rising ahead, fork up left at a cairn to a smaller path. This follows the slightly rocky ridgeline,

Heading up the northwest ridge to Y Lliwedd

with great views to the crags on the left. Rejoin the main path briefly, but before it turns off steeply downhill (it's the Watkin Path) head off up the front face of Y Lliwedd. Here there is a scree path zigzagging up among the crags. Scramblers will keep as far up left as possible, overlooking the northern crags, with some easy scrambling. A cairn marks the higher west summit of **Y Lliwedd**, with a nice ridge path round to the 893m east top.

The ridge path heads down, sometimes on the south (right-hand) flank, to a flat boggy shoulder at 700m altitude. At the left edge of this plateau, a cairn (SH631535) marks the top of the descent path, a steep zig-zag of scree on bare rock. Its lowest part is pitched path.

The path continues down to a hut at a corner of **Llyn Llydaw**. Here turn right along the smooth Miners Track. It contours above **Llyn Teyrn** and round the base of a hill spur, then into the car park at Pen y Pass.

3

The Welsh Three Thousands

by Roy Clayton

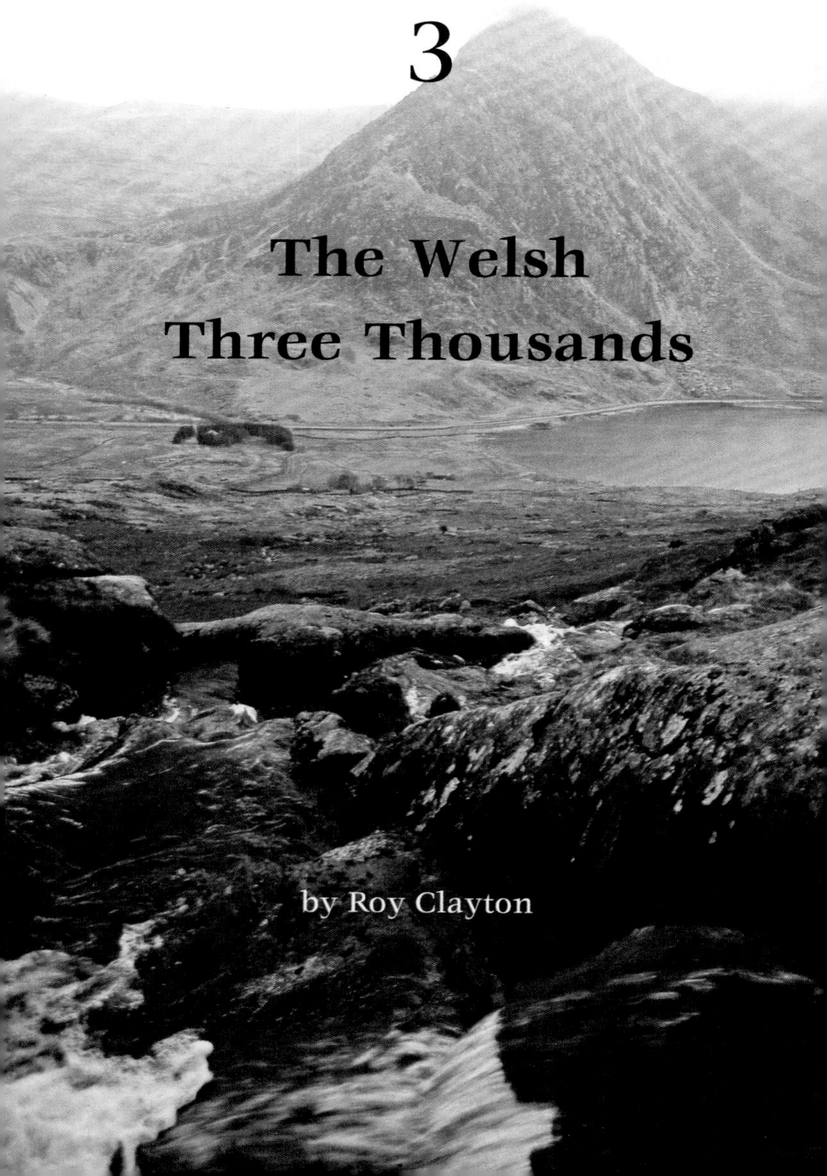

The Welsh 3000s
History and Records
by Harvey Lloyd

Who it was that first donned his boots and set off for the summit of Yr Wyddfa with the intentions of traversing the Welsh three thousand foot peaks in one go is lost in the history of mountaineering. It would probably be in Victorian times, perhaps from a small hotel such as the Pen y Gwryd or Gorphwysfa (Pen y Pass). It is recorded that Eustace Thomas of the Manchester-based Rucksack Club walked it in 1919 with a group of friends. His time, twenty-two and a half hours, seems unremarkable enough but, considering he had passed his fiftieth birthday, had been described as an ageing business man with a weak digestion, troublesome feet and the beginnings of an elderly spread, and had not taken up long distance walking until the previous year, it becomes more creditable.

The walker of his time had none of today's high tech gear. Heavy boots, tweeds, poor waterproofs and little equipment were balanced, however, by a great enthusiasm for the hills and the challenge they presented. These men were true pioneers!

In the early days the route followed was nearly as variable as the time taken. Parties started from Nant Gwynant, Llanberis, Pen y Gwryd and Aber. The idea of starting and finishing at the same place to make a round trip with no transport problems was soon adopted, the Llanberis or Ogwen Valleys being the main starting/finishing points. The Locked Book at the Pen y Gwryd Hotel is a mine of information on these early attempts. Many visitors to this hotel took on board the traverse of the Welsh 3's. They realised that there was a record to be broken in addition to the pleasure of a long day on the hills. Philips and Clay managed to fit in a hearty breakfast at the P-y-G and a forty minute tea-stop at Ogwen Cottage in a trip that took seventeen hours.

Opposite: Tryfan and the head of Llyn Ogwen, from Afon Lloer

Herbert Carr, in The Mountains of Snowdonia, published in 1925, must have been instrumental in encouraging many of the early attempts. He wrote:

"Strong walkers will not visit Snowdonia many times without wishing to include the Carnedds, the Glyders and Snowdon in a single expedition. It is a very fine walk and, under favourable conditions, very well worth doing. In length it is about thirty miles when taken from Beddgelert, Conwy or Llanfairfechan. From thirteen to fourteen hours may be allowed, halts included, at an ordinary pace. It can be reduced by making the Ogwen Valley and Pen y Pass the points of departure and arrival. If part of the walk has to be done in the dark it is best to reserve the paths of Snowdon for the night watches. A moon, preferably full, is to be desired."

Carr does not tell us if he attempted the walk himself but he was obviously writing to the 'hard men' of the twenties.

By the thirties the writer Showell Styles had finished the route in twelve hours forty-four minutes and then Frank Shuttleworth achieved ten hours twenty-nine minutes.

Thomas Firbank set the scene for the post Second World War upsurge in interest. A fascinating account of his own record attempt is given in his book I Bought a Mountain. He colourfully described the rigorous training he and his wife Esmé adopted for the event. They looked for ways to modify the route and came up with the idea of descending Crib Goch's north ridge, thus saving valuable miles.

In the Spring of 1938, the well publicised record attempt took place and the roadsides of Nant Peris were lined with spectators. On the summit of Snowdon the newspapermen were gathered in anticipation of a new record. The competitors were regally conveyed to the summit by a specially laid on train. Thomas Firbank did set the record along with companions W.E. Capel Cure and R.M. Hamer, reaching Foel-fras in a time of eight hours and twenty-five minutes. Esmé, accompanied by Thomas Davies and hampered by a foot injury, limped home in an equally impressive time of nine hours twenty-nine minutes. Firbank prophesied that one day somebody would complete the journey in seven and a half hours but not much faster!

Firbank's successful attempt brought to the forefront the simmering controversy that had been around for some time: should the mountaineer run in the mountains? The attempt was frowned upon by the establishment and resulted in an apology by Firbank's companions being published in the Climbers' Club Journal for 1939. There was no doubt that it was not the done thing for members of the club to take part in such escapades that produce "some rather unwelcome publicity in the press".

The fifties brought the athletes to the hills. John Disley set seven hours twenty-four minutes, then a group including Bertie Robertson and Chris Brasher clocked six hours dead. The sixties saw Eric Beard home in the 'impossible' time of five hours thirteen minutes. Just before his untimely death in a car crash in 1969, 'Beardie' had been on a training run with a friend, Joss Naylor, who he predicted would take his records. On a damp, misty June morning in 1973 this shepherd from Wasdale took up that offer and set off from the summit of Snowdon. It was only the fourth time he had been to Wales, and he became cragfast on the damp rocks of Crib Goch. "Thirty-five minutes to the road," he records with a hint of dissatisfaction. Unfamiliarity led him to a poor route up Glyder Fach's summit boulderpile. On Carnedd Llewelyn he lost more time and only the appearance of three Welshmen out of the mist saved him from going seriously astray. But four hours forty-six minutes after leaving Snowdon's summit, still in mist, he touched the summit of Foel-fras. Joss's verdict: there's about ten minutes to come off that time.

The record was to stand until 1988 when Colin Donnelly, a member of the Eryri Harriers, recorded an unbelievable four hours nineteen minutes, including Carnedd Uchaf, a new summit added to the earlier list of fourteen by the latest Ordnance Survey maps. Colin was accompanied and paced by his team-mates from the Harriers. Donnelly, like Naylor, wasn't entirely happy with his run. "Shouldn't have been so tired on the Carneddau, really should have knocked a further ten minutes off." Perhaps someone reading this book will prove Donnelly wrong with his ten minutes – as Joss Naylor, John Barford, Thomas Firbank have all been wrong before him – and take the Welsh Three Thousands record below four hours. But it seems more likely that this outstanding run, unbeaten now for 20 full years, will remain so for a similarly long time to come.

The females too have left their mark with some very creditable times. Angela Carson ran five hours twenty-eight minutes in 1989 to put herself in the record books.

An event of this nature holds glory for all that take part. The group of schoolboys that accomplished a complete round of the 3000's from Pen y Gwryd with Dr G. Linsey Jones in sixteen hours two minutes must have been very pleased with themselves, and one wonders how John Wagstaff felt in 1978 after completing the route three times in twenty-two hours forty-nine minutes.

The Fifteenth Threethousander

Until 1984 there were only 14 Welsh 3000s. Thomas Firbank and Joss Naylor both left Carnedd Uchaf unvisited. This was nothing to do with subtle reckoning of drops to cols. Rather, we realise with surprise just how unreliable Ordnance Survey mapping was, as recently as thirty years ago.

The old-style one-inch Snowdonia map has the highest contour of Carnedd Uchaf at 2950ft. McKnight Docharty, who listed the 2000ft hills in 1962, noted that the mapping of Carnedd Uchaf was incorrect and that it was actually at least 3000ft high. Nevertheless, the first metric mapping, of 1977, had the same top contour line, now relabelled as 899m. The first metric survey of 1983, and its map published in 1984, at last gave Carnedd Uchaf its 926m spot height.

And now in 2009, this hill has acquired a new name to go with its new altitude. Follwing agitations by the Princess Gwenllian Sociecty, Carnedd (or Garnedd) Uchaf now is also known as Carnedd Gwenllian. Daughter of Prince Llewelyn and sister of Dafydd, Gwenllian was capured by the English as an infant and spent her obscure life confined in

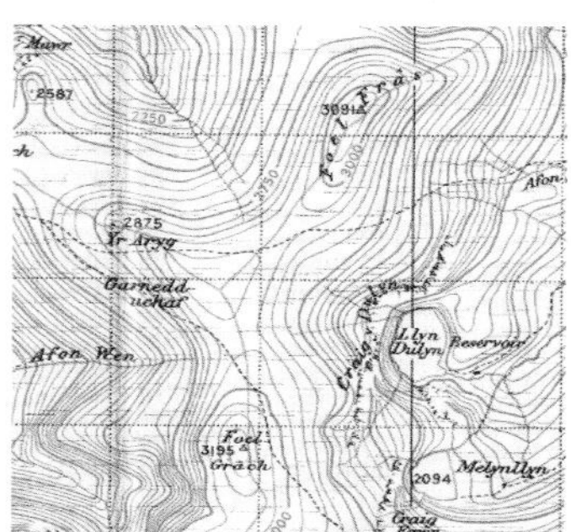

One-inch Ordnance Survey map from the 1950's, showing Carnedd Uchaf without ts top contour

a nunnery. So far the Big Mac Appreciation Society has been unsuccessful in its lobbying to have Snowdon renamed as Carnedd y Hambyrgyr.

If Wales were ever conquered by the Scots (I know, the Welsh warriors are far too fierce for that), how many of the fifteen Welsh 3000s would be added into Munro's Tables? The Tables do in fact list 3000-footers outside Scotland, in a category called 'Furth of Scotland'. This has 13 pseudo-Munros in Wales, excluding only Carnedd Ugain and Foel Grach.

More intriguingly, John and Jean Nuttall, whose book *The Mountains of England & Wales* lists every Welsh Peak with 50ft

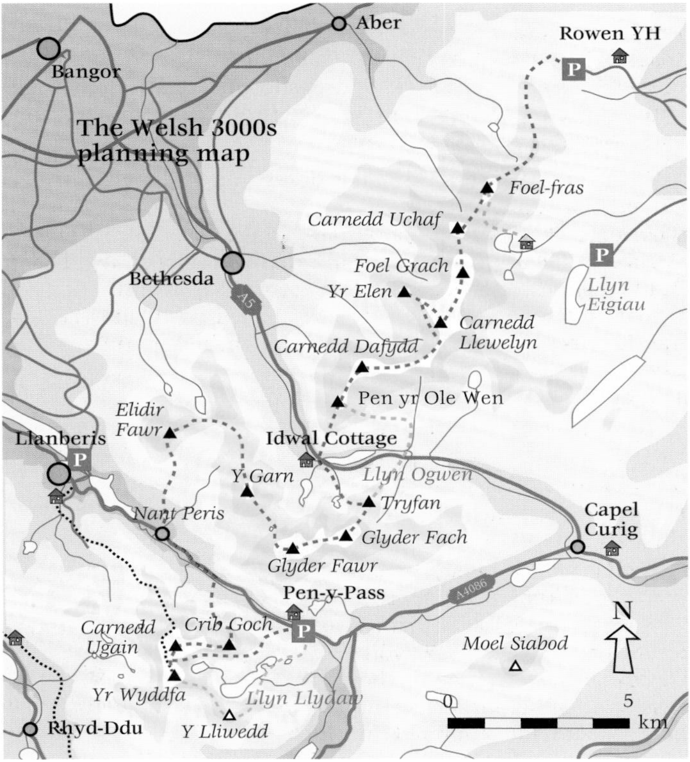

of drop around it, measured Castell y Gwynt, between the two Glyders, as very nearly another Welsh 3000-footer. Their initial survey, using clinometer, surveying pole, and John Nuttall himself who is exactly 6ft tall, determined the drop around Castell y Gwynt at 49.5ft. But in 2007, precision levelling using a laser measuring device by John Barnard and Graham Jackson has given it 51.5ft of drop – possibly the col has eroded by being walked and even camped on over 20 years. We don't consider even 51.5ft (15.7m) enough for it to count as a separate mountain and the 16th 3000er. Nevertheless, visiting its spiky top adds a pleasant (and in wind and wet quite challenging) scrambling moment to the Welsh 3000s walk, and doesn't take any longer than going around.

As we go to press, spoilsport surveyors are remeasuring Tryfan. If they should discover it to be below 3000ft (the odds are they won't), this is one update we shall ***not*** incorporate. Losing Tryfan, Wales' finest mountain, would make the 3000s walk shorter, but also considerably less superb. And whether above or below 914.4m, Tryfan for us will always be a Three-thousander.

THE SNOWDON GROUP

Snowdon summit: Yr Wyddfa (the grave or tumulus)	3560ft (1085m)
Carnedd Ugain (twentieth cairn)	3493ft (1065m)
Crib Goch (red crest – Crib is literally a comb)	3027ft (924m)

Wales' mountains are firmly routed in its culture and heritage and none more so than Snowdon, the principality's highest summit and also the highest south of the Scottish border. The Snowdon group consists of five major peaks. Yr Wyddfa is the more acceptable Welsh name for Snowdon itself, and is used in this book to designate the summit pyramid. Carnedd Ugain is misspelt as Garnedd Ugain on current OS maps. Crib y Ddysgl (ridge of the dish), the only name given on older maps and on Harveys, is actually the mountain's rocky east ridge. The other three are Crib Goch, Y Lliwedd and Yr Aran.

Y Lliwedd, Crib Goch, Yr Wyddfa and Carnedd Ugain, from Glyder Fawr

Yr Wyddfa has, in terms of mountain architecture, few peers within the United Kingdom. Its pointed summit is guarded by precipitous cliffs and, not surprisingly, affords one of the most spectacular panoramas in all of Wales. This includes the wide sweep of Cardigan Bay and the northern coastline. On a good day you can see four countries from the summit cairn: Scotland, Ireland, England and of course Wales. Mind you, it has to be a very good day indeed to see Merrick in the Galloway Hills of Scotland: at 144 miles (232km) this is the longest viewable distance in the UK. I am usually happy to see my hands and feet. A dozen or so lakes and tarns of various sizes glint in the valleys and cwms. Dominant among these is Llyn Llydaw, which fills the huge Cwm Dyli.

Many people felt Snowdon had been spoilt by the construction of the railway and summit cafe. Prince Charles called it 'the highest slum in Wales'. I certainly despised it when arriving hot and bothered ten minutes after closing time.

On 12 June 2009 the new Summit Café, affectionately referred to as the Pill Box, opened for business. The swish new interior is reminiscent of a Swedish sauna, except for the dress code of course. It is much smaller than the previous building and can get a little crowded in the summer. The new building cost £8.3 million (they should make it back on the tea), and houses an information centre, a cafe and a shelter. The only casualty is the bar – call that progress! Mind you, it has to be said that beer and mountains don't mix. I recall a hot summer day when after a couple pints at the summit cafe, I wagered I could beat the train down to Llanberis. Although I won my bet I spent so much time on my backside that I arrived at the station with bruises blacker than a Carneddau cloud. For me, fell running and 'fell over' are closely related concepts.

The 2ft 7in gauge rack railway was opened in 1896 and had a tragic accident on the first day. On the descent a train was derailed and tumbled down the mountainside, narrowly missing several climbers. One person died – a passenger who leapt out of a moving carriage. The trains, some of them the originals, have since carried millions of joyful travellers to the rooftop of Wales and some less joyful ones to Clogwyn. To some, myself included, it is comforting to see the plumes of smoke from the little steam engines billowing from the high ridges, or the sound of their hoots echoing through the clinging mists.

Crib Goch and its pinnacles are undoubtedly the most exhilarating part of the Three Thousands. I vividly remember my first visit. The cloud base was barely over fifteen hundred feet and wispy grey mist swirled around my feet as I trod gingerly over the damp rock of the crest. It was an eerie experience and I could only imagine the drop through the clouds to the valley below. I have since introduced many friends to this superb and spectacular ridge. Some are still friends today!

Ghostly relics of the old copper mines and quarries litter many routes to the top. In legend, King Arthur fought with the treacherous Sir Mordred at Cwm Tregalan (south of the summit). In the bloody battle Arthur forced his foe into a retreat up the mountain to the pass between Yr Wyddfa and Y Lliwedd, but was hit by an arrow. Before dying, he slew Sir Mordred with the mighty sword Excalibur. The place has been known since as Bwlch y Saethau (Pass of the Arrows).

Beneath Bwlch y Saethau lies Glaslyn. Romantics believe that in its bottomless depths lives a fearsome monster called Afanc. This beast formerly lived in Llyn-yr-Afanc, near Betws-y-Coed, where he would often create severe floods. After one particularly bad wetting, Afanc's neighbours decided to act.

They knew this beast had an eye for the ladies, and with the help of a beautiful damsel lured him from the pool, while they hid behind the bushes. As the amorous monster made his appearance the villagers set on him. After binding poor Afanc in chains they dragged him across mountains and valleys before dumping him into Glaslyn. (The whole event must have been a bit like a stag night in Blackpool.) Some say he lives there still. Other less romantic souls say he was just a beaver. Well, you know how these Welshmen exaggerate!

SNOWDON the route

Yr Wyddfa (Snowdon) to Nant Peris

4 1/2 miles (6.5km) height gain: 200m

After taking a last look from Yr Wyddfa's summit SH609543 (starting at the trig point of course), the marathon begins. Descend in a north-northwest direction, keeping to the path close to the edge of the huge corrie of Cwm Dyli and parallel to the mountain railway. The descending path has been greatly improved in the last few years and so Bwlch Glas, the pass between Yr Wyddfa and Carnedd Ugain, is soon reached. The spot is marked by the 'Pigtop Pillar', a huge obelisk where walkers using both the Miners and Pig Tracks gain the ridge. The obtrusive obelisk was erected by the National Park to provide a waymark when winter snows lie deep.

Beyond the obelisk, a sprawling cairn marks the departure of the popular Llanberis path. Our route veers slightly to the right, still keeping to the edge of Cwm Dyli. The wide, cairned path affords an easy pace as it climbs towards Carnedd Ugain SH610551, whose grassy top is crowned by a flaking white trig point. Two peaks scaled in a matter of minutes! It's easy stuff this peak bagging! Although the views to Llanberis and the Glyders are striking, the knife-edged ridge to the Pinnacles of Crib Goch captures most attention.

On the way down Carnedd Ugain you are confronted by a choice of well-worn paths. This can be confusing in mist. It is advisable to maintain an easterly direction, close to the edge of

Snowdon Range: 1
YrWyddfa to Crib Goch

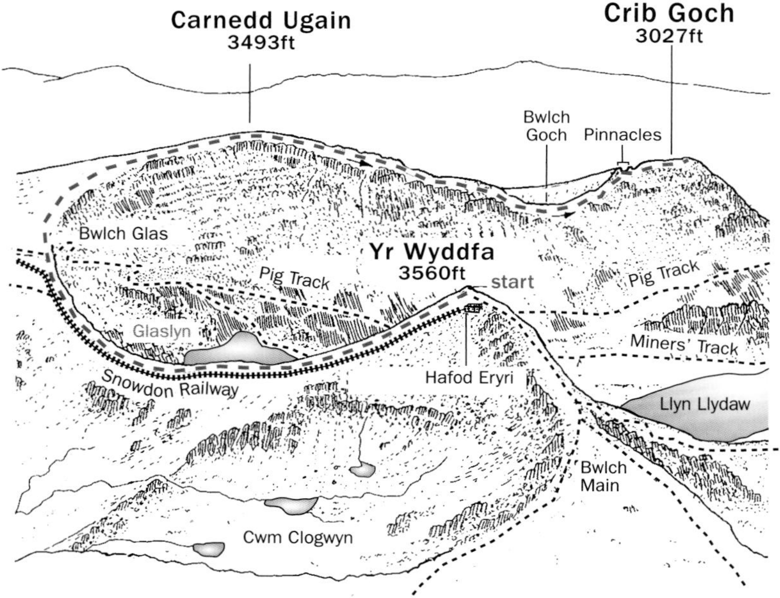

Cwm Dyli, as this is where the path materialises when the ridge narrows.

After dropping into a hollow the crest of the ridge is followed before veering a few feet to the left of a rocky buttress. In favourable conditions the arete itself is the finest course as the climber is challenged to clamber over half a mile of rocky bluffs and clefts. The use of hands and occasionally bottoms will be needed here. The course ceases to be obvious as the ridge appears to terminate abruptly at a cliff face. A path is available to the right however. The ridge continues rocky to the broad grassy pass, Bwlch Goch 858m (marked Coch on current maps)..

The lofty crests of the Crib Goch Pinnacles, which now lie ahead, form the most demanding obstacle of the route.

The most satisfying way is the one over the knife-edged crest, although this is very exposed and not suitable for those with a nervous disposition or on a bicycle. This higher route starts its ascent on the right hand side of the first pinnacle, where a steep path quickly attains the top. Shuffle along a narrow shelf before dropping down the left side to the depression.
The easier way contours around this first pinnacle on its right (Llyn Llydaw) side. Head up the pinnacle about half way, where it steepens. Now a rock ledge contours round to the right, taking you across the rock face to the stony gully behind the pinnacle. Head left, up this, to its top.

The second pinnacle is tackled from the left side. Continue along the ridge for about 200 metres to a pile of stones marking Crib Goch's true summit (923m at SH624551). *Here see Variation S2, on page 79, which requires steps to be retraced along the Pinnacles to Bwlch Goch – for fast running times only.*

This is exciting stuff – Snowdonia is laid beneath your feet. Teasing glimpses of Cwm Uchaf and Llyn Glas add to the drama of the situation. The next stage is the narrowest of all. The good

Looking back to Crib Goch, from Cwm Glas

Snowdon 2
Crib Goch to Blaen-y-nant

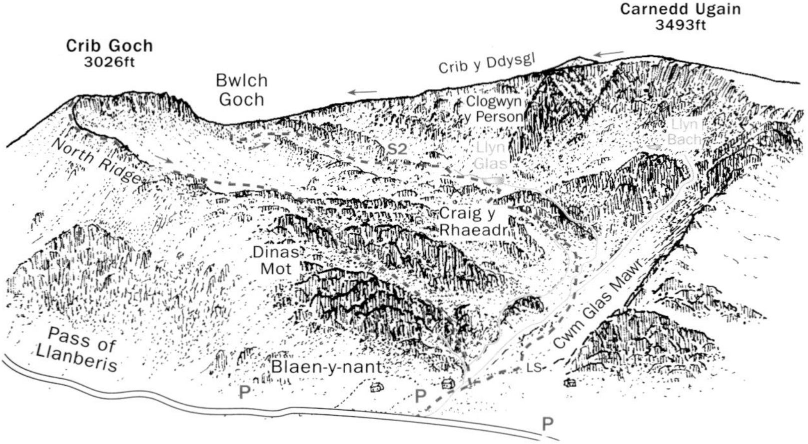

scrambling is on blocky rocks immediately below and to the right of the crest, which is used as a handrail. There is also an exposed, gravelly path a few metres further down to the right.

Crib Goch's more celebrated North Summit (921m) is marked by a polished circular rock platform and a meeting of ridges.

Most walkers will descend Crib Goch eastwards by way of Bwlch Moch to their journey's end at Pen y Pass, but the Welsh 3000s is barely started. Here the excitement continues on the arete which curves northwards, forming the right-hand edge of rugged Cwm Uchaf. Care needs to be exercised on this exposed spur, as the rock is not as secure as it was on the well-trodden Crib Goch Pinnacles.

At the end of the rocky section the ridge funnels you sharply down the pinkish screes, descending northwest on a loose scree path. Continuing northwards on the most direct line would bring you to the vast cliffs of Dinas Mot below (not good). Continue northwest down a grassy little valley to reach a wet, grassy bowl fringed by rock outcrops. From here a stream descends in waterfalls (SH 6221 5618) with a small path scrambling down its right (east) side (*water source*). This stream is not marked at all on Landranger maps. It leads into Cwm Glas Mawr beneath the huge rocky knoll of Dinas Mot.

From the waterfall's foot keep ahead above a broken wall, passing below a damp black overhang, to cross a larger stream. Turn down to the right to a stile, before crossing a bridge over the Afon Gennog to the left of the farm at Blaen-y-nant (SH 6230 5697).

The twisting narrow road is then followed for 2km (1 1/2 miles) to the little village of Nant Peris. There is parking here for those lucky people with friends in support, as well as a telephone box in the village to summon a taxi if you've had enough.

Above the Pass of Llanberis on the descent from Cwm Glas

THE GLYDERAU (Glyders)	
Glyder Fawr (Big Lump)	3279ft (999m)
Glyder Fach (Little Mound)	3262ft (994m)
Y Garn (The Cairn)	3107ft (947m)
Elidir Fawr The seldom-used correct name for this mountain is Carnedd Elidir	3029ft (923m)
Tryfan (Three Peaks)	3002ft (915m)

From Capel Curig westwards stretches a ten mile range of compressed and slaty volcanic rocks that has long been my favourite tramping ground. The Glyderau, or Glyders, include some of Wales' most rugged peaks and issue a stern challenge for the hardiest walker. Five of our 3000-footers are located here. The Glyders' northern faces above Ogwen are bold, with deeply gouged cwms and sculpted cliffs and crags. Several of those cwms contain delightful tarns.

Highest of the range, although only by a few feet, is Glyder Fawr, a rugged mountain with a large summit plateau of splintered rock and several menacing outcrops. The terrain is not unlike the surface of the moon. Glyder Fawr's next door neighbour, Glyder Fach has even more spectacular features. Castell y Gwynt (Castle of the Winds) is a gaunt and massive outcrop thrown together like a crudely built dry-stone wall. It forms a formidable obstacle to walkers from Glyder Fawr – most walk around its base though pedantic peakbaggers as well as those who fancy a small scramble will clamber across it (just head straight up the front). The Cantilever slab, set slightly beyond the summit, seems precariously perched on an offset fulcrum. In fact it has been there for thousands of years and has withstood the weight of the many travellers posing for their 'all conquering' summit snapshots. They bounce around gleefully trying to move the immovable, like a child sharing a seesaw with a large grownup. But Glyder Fach's most powerful feature has to be the Bristly Ridge. This jagged spur, which affords an excellent scramble, plummets towards Bwlch Tryfan.

Looking from Glyder Fawr onwards towards Glyder Fach

This brings us to my favourite mountain, Tryfan, a magnificent wedge-shaped peak slightly out on a limb from the main ridge. It towers over Ogwen, proudly boasting of its buttresses and gullies to all who venture along the A5 highway to Holyhead. Tryfan has been likened to a shark's fin or to a gigantic Stegosaurus. Is it just the women who see it as a giant Toblerone? A little hard to swallow methinks! Tryfan may only be the smallest of the 3000s, but as the writer Steve Ashton says: "There's nothing only about Tryfan." View Ogwen Mountain Rescue's callout maps (www.ogwen-rescue.org.uk) to see how many have underestimated Tryfan.

Standing on the shores of Llyn Ogwen, you cannot fail to be impressed by the bold facade of Y Garn, the mountain on the western skyline. Y Garn exudes the nobility of a robed elder surveying the Ogwen valley. It is strange to discover, however, that it has a soft side, for once on the summit you can see its grassy southern slopes declining gently towards Nant Peris. In fact, with the exception of Esgair Felen, which towers above the boulder gorge of the Pass of Llanberis, the southern slopes of all the Glyders are more gentle than their northern ones.

The southern slopes of Elidir Fawr have been scarred by the vast quarries of Dinorwig to reveal terraces of bare rock and

Glyderau 1
Blaen-y-nant to Llyn y Cwn

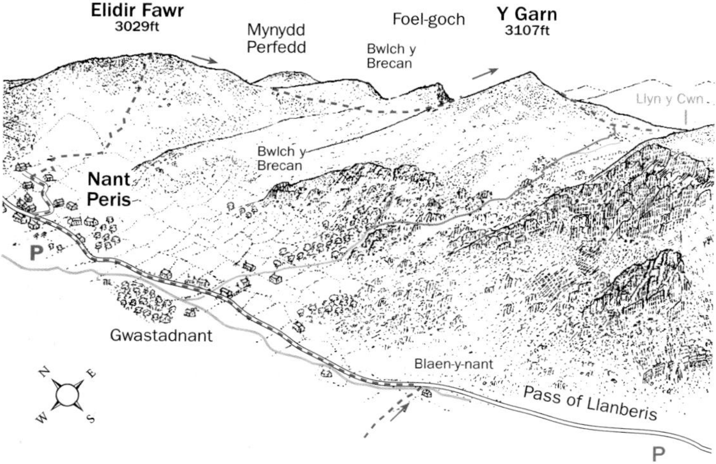

barren slag heaps. This rocky-topped crest, the most remote of the three thousands, holds secrets, for hidden inside it are the workings of a pumped-storage power station. The 1728MW station, which is built into the mountainside by the shores of Llyn Peris, was opened in 1984 at a cost of £450 million. It was then the largest of its type in the world. At times of peak demand for electricity (e.g. at breakfast) water from the Marchlyn Mawr Reservoir is released through tunnels down 600m to power the six turbines. At times of low demand the turbines are reversed and water is pumped back up to Marchlyn Mawr, thus restoring levels, which can vary by over 50 metres.

The GLYDERAU the route

Nant Peris to Idwal Cottage (Ogwen Valley)

15.5km (9 1/2 miles) height gain: 1800m

The next stage of the route leaves **Nant Peris** via a walled lane, sandwiched between the chapel and Ty Isaf campsite. Pass the campsite entrance and follow the public footpath sign left along the narrow lane past the whitewashed cottage of Cerrig Dryddion to reach Nant yr Fron. To the left of Nant yr Fron cross a ladder stile and continue along the lane for a further 30 metres to an anorexic looking metal farm gate on the right. Go through the gate then head up to the top left corner of the field and another stile adjacent to a rickety iron gate.

The path zigzags uphill in delightful fields of bracken and foxgloves to reach a **footbridge** (SH 6086 5958). Elidir Fawr lies directly ahead, its quarry-scarred, grassy facade soaring from the Afon Dudodyn *(water source*) to its craggy crest.

Leave the path to cross the bridge where an obvious track begins the tortuous slog northwards climbing a steep, crag-interspersed, grassy slope. A narrow but well worn path heads towards the first of three erosion control fences (SH 6090 6013), which are extremely useful for route finding. After scaling a stile over the fence and the adjacent cross-wall it is best to rake across the grassy slopes northeast. This area is quite spongy and the path appears to have absconded. The key is to locate the second fence at SH 6092 6045 after which the path reappears. Strike uphill immediately behind the second fence to the last fence at the 600m contour (SH 6094 6053). Here you can usually feel the fresh breezes sweeping over the col ahead, and soon the view opens out to reveal Foel Goch and Y Garn across the deep and desolate hollow of the Afon Dudodyn. The fragmented crest of Esgair Felen overshadows the cleft of the Llanberis Pass. The path rakes parallel to the river, to the base of Elidir Fawr's rocky crest. A vigorous final assault now begins over boulder-ridden slopes to **Elidir Fawr's** hard won summit. The path arrives rather unexpectedly at the summit wind shelter (SH 6120 6130).

The comforting wind-shelter is a fine place to linger if you're not racing against the clock. To the northwest, beyond Marchlyn Bach and its craggy amphitheatre, Bangor and the Menai Straits lie beyond a flat, chequered pastureland speckled with trees, houses and rivers. To the south all but the very top of Snowdon is shielded by the protective arm of Clogwyn.

Leave **Elidir's** summit in a north-easterly direction on an initially rocky descent, aided by a few cairns. This soon transforms into a broad path on a grassy ridge, which, in turn, narrows into a rocky ridge with steep drops to the left. Marchlyn Mawr is framed beautifully from here – quite a spectacle if you are partial to nature being corrupted by symmetrical concrete shorelines. The route arcs round the grassy chasm of Cwm Dudodyn to **Bwlch y Brecan**, south of Mynydd Perfedd (the 'Mountain of the Entrails' – perhaps it takes some guts to get there?) Here you can look down over the deep valley of Nant Ffrancon, which divides the Glyders from the Carneddau. The precipitous rugged slopes of Pen yr Ole Wen give a hint of the challenge yet to come. To the left a stile marks the first of several seductive escape routes. This one leads very steeply down to Nant Ffrancon.

Those in a hurry will choose to omit Foel-goch. Fine peak though it is, it fails to reach that three thousand foot figure, and a good level path obliges by traversing the southern slopes, rejoining the ridge above Cwm Cywion.

There is now a clear wide path contouring along a terrace high above Afon Dudodyn – you often feel that it is heading too close to the Llanberis valley. Little height is gained until a fence and stile are reached (SH 6266 6036) over 2km from Elidir's top.

Here Y Garn begins to imposes itself. A worn gritty path zigzagging steeply passes several large cairns before reaching **Y Garn's** summit, which boasts one of the finest views in Wales. From here the lakes of Llyn Peris, Ogwen, Bochlwyd, Idwal and Y Garn's own attendant tarn, Llyn Clyd, are all visible, studded in a rugged mountainscape that includes the serrated tops and

Y Garn and Llyn y Cwn from the long, stony slope of Glyder Fawr

tremendous cliffs of Glyders Fawr and Fach, and the reptilian facade of Tryfan.

From Y Garn there are initially two paths of descent towards Llyn y Cwn. The more entertaining one stays closer to the cliff edge. Both are usable and converge beyond a fence with two stiles a few yards apart. As the path nears the desolate small tarn (Llyn y Cwn) the terrain becomes boggier. Here the path is joined by one that has come up from Ogwen and the Devil's Kitchen, and that makes another tempting escape for the footsore and weary. From the southern tip of the lake another escape route to the right leads back to Gwastadnant in the Llanberis valley. That route is steep but spectacular, and offers unsurpassed views of Snowdon – well worth a return visit.

Passing **Llyn y Cwn** (*water source – last until Ogwen*) on the left bank, go round a rocky knoll before forgeing mercilessly upwards towards Glyder Fawr. There are several ways but the best one begins slightly to the left of a stony gully as it climbs some 250m. The slippery shale path, which is dangerous in wintry conditions, eases in the later stages as it zigzags to the

Glyderau 2
Llyn y Cwn to Ogwen

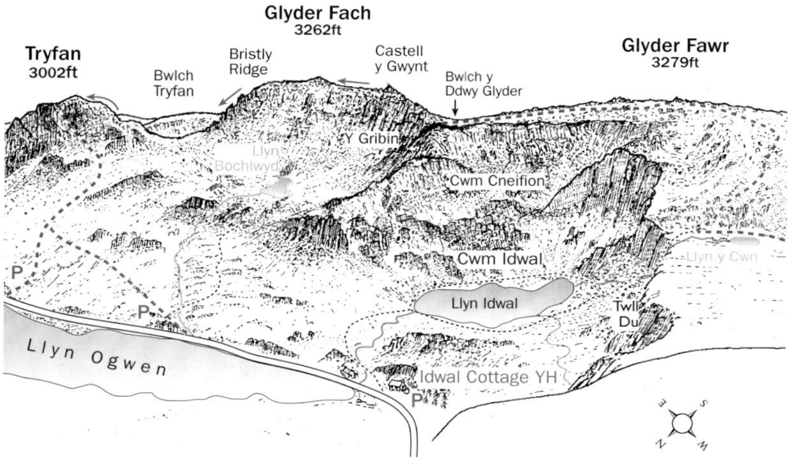

barren plateau. There are several pretentious summits, but after a little head scratching you should eventually work out that a particularly large one marks the summit of **Glyder Fawr,** three-thousand footer number six (SH642579). The path dissects the two rocky protrusions and there is a small but welcome wind shelter to the left.

The connecting path to Glyder Fach is an entertaining stroll. The proliferation of cairns makes navigation easy in clear conditions but a little confusing in hill fog. The views down the Nameless Cwm to the left are breathtaking as a huge wall of rock, Clogwyn Du, plunges 600m into a craggy abyss with Llyn Idwal basking in its rugged cwm far below. On the opposite side, the heather-clad, stony southern slopes of Glyder Fach decline more gently to Llyn Cwmffynnon and Pen y Gwryd.

Beyond **Bwlch y Ddwy Glyder** the route is confronted by **Castell y Gwynt** (Castle of the Winds SH 6542 5824), a juxtaposition of sharp rocks some 60m in height. Practised scramblers can tackle them directly. It is easier however to pass

The Cantilever slab on the summit plateau of Glyder Fach

to the right of them, although this does involve a little loss of height and some grappling with bouldery slopes.

You are now on **Glyder Fach**'s summit plateau: another that has been likened to a lunar landscape. The actual summit (SH 6565 5830) is formed by a massive pile of boulders with deep crevices waiting to swallow up the unsuspecting. Continuing eastwards the route passes to left of the **Cantilever** (SH 6575 5832), a giant slab precariously perched on a rock outcrop often elusive in mist. On most occasions walkers will be posing for pictures.

Bearing northeast from the Cantilever, a large obtrusion of rock is the top of the Bristly Ridge and marks the start of the route to our eighth peak, Tryfan. Care should be taken in mist as there are dangerous precipices to the left before you reach this point. Bristly Ridge itself is a time-consuming rock scramble better in ascent, and thus the best course is from a sprawling cairn (SH 6594 5840) down the scree slopes to its right (east). They are steep and eroded and care should be taken, especially in snow or ice. Pass directly downhill in the wide, open gully, then slant down left along the base of Bristly Ridge, before following a wall down across the pass **Bwlch Tryfan**.

Cross any of several ladder stiles in the pass. (An escape path now descends left to Llyn Bochlwyd.) Keep ahead along the wall

Looking across Bwlch Tryfan to Tryfan, from the stony descent off Glyder Fach

towards Tryfan's **Far South Peak**. Take this direct for some worthwhile scrambling, possibly up to Grade 2, on good rock. Or skirt well to left on an ascending spiral, worn path with some bouldery clambering. Above and behind the Far South Peak, a col on your right has a short wall across and a ladder stile (which you would cross to descend Heather Terrace). Easiest is to keep across to the left of this col, on worn path and bouldery clambers; a more direct line straight up offers more scrambling of good quality with many routes. A final slight dip is crossed to the twin rock pillars of **Tryfan** summit (SH664593).

The two pillars on Tryfan's diminutive but airy summit are known as Adam and Eve. Presumably Adam is the more portly of the two stones. In the true traditions of temptation many are coaxed into jumping the gap between the two to earn the 'freedom of Tryfan'.

Sensible walkers will resist the temptation as little is achieved and one slip would signal the end of the journey. But anyway here is a photo of the author enjoying the jump. Oops!

There are several options from the top of Tryfan. The steep descent by the West Gully is the quickest: in a popular fell race, times of under seven minutes have been recorded from summit to the shores of Ogwen! The North Ridge, directly ahead, is a very entertaining Grade 1 scramble, but eats deeply into the time schedule and is more difficult when taken downhill. The quickest descent is described below, but at the end of this chapter are two noteworthy alternatives. A return to Bwlch Tryfan is only slightly slower and offers an easier and less eroded path *(see Variant G1 on page 80)*. A descent by Heather Terrace is quite a bit slower but is, except to the seriously exhausted, really enjoyable *(Variant G2, page 81)*.

But for the quick **West Gully** descent a course should be set northwards over worn ground towards a secondary peak (Tryfan North Peak). From a point just down to the left of the first col a well-used (over-used) path descends an open gully to the left (west), mercilessly steep but not scrambly.

As the slope opens out, the path, now rebuilt in stone chunks, heads north-northwest down steep but safer grassy slopes, with the crest of the north ridge well to the right. At the foot of this, as the slope eases at about the 400m contour, the path divides.

If you intend to use the 'fast' route up Pen yr Ole Wen's south ridge, fork left on a faint grass path. This heads down a gentle spurline to the foot of the stream below Llyn Bochlwyd. Cross a ladder stile (SH653603) onto the A5 and follow pavement to Ogwen Cottage (Outdoor Centre) and Idwal Cottage Youth Hostel, where there are toilets, a refreshment kiosk, a telephone box and a car park.

The opposite direction should be chosen for the increasingly popular east ridge *(Variant C1 on page 82)*. Fork right on a small path that meanders amongst grass and crag to reach Ogwen's shores at a roadside car park; and turn right.

THE CARNEDDAU (Carnedds)	
Carnedd Llewelyn (Llewelyn's Cairn)	**1064m (3484ft)**
Carnedd Dafydd (David's Cairn)	**1044m (3426ft)**
Pen yr Ole Wen (Hill of the White Light)	**978m (3210ft)**
Foel Grach (Scabby Hill)	**976m (3195ft)**
Yr Elen (Helen, or from gelen, Leech)	**962m (3152ft)**
Foel-fras (Broad Hill)	**942m (3091ft)**
Carnedd Uchaf (Highest Cairn) also named as Carnedd Gwenllian	**926m (3038ft)**

When approached on the A55 coast road to Conwy, the ruffled edge of Tal y Fan signals the beginning of the high Carneddau. This remote range of mountains rises from the Irish Sea, spreading southwards into the heart of Snowdonia.

The northern Carneddau consist of whaleback ridges and rounded hills, clad with grass, scattered with boulders and dissected by clear, cool mountain streams. In the loftier southern peaks, rock surfaces more frequently as cliffs such as Carnedd Dafydd's Ysgolion Duon (the Black Ladders) and Llewelyn's

Pen yr Ole Wen, from the slopes of Tryfan

Craig yr Ysfa. Llewelyn himself was the last independent Prince of Wales, betrayed (by the people of Builth Wells) to Edward I of England in 1282. His brother Dafydd was hanged, drawn and quartered at Shrewsbury. This may put the sufferings of the hillwalker on these final hills into perspective.

The Carneddau's last sentinel, Pen yr Ole Wen, watches over Ogwen where, in one swoop, craggy, scree-strewn slopes plummet over six hundred metres. Between north and south is an area as wild and remote as any in Snowdonia – one not unlike the Cairngorms of Scotland.

In good weather the free-striding, broad ridges between Pen yr Ole Wen and Foel-fras are a delight, but in misty conditions route-finding can be difficult, especially in the region of Foel Grach. Once upon a time Foel Grach's hut had an interesting visitor's book, and judging by stories in the refuge shelter many walkers have had narrow escapes. On my first visit to the shelter I met a retired gentleman from the Conway valley who climbed the mountain almost every day to replenish emergency food and water supplies. Nowadays the cupboard is bare, but

Carneddau 1
Ogwen to Carnedd Dafydd

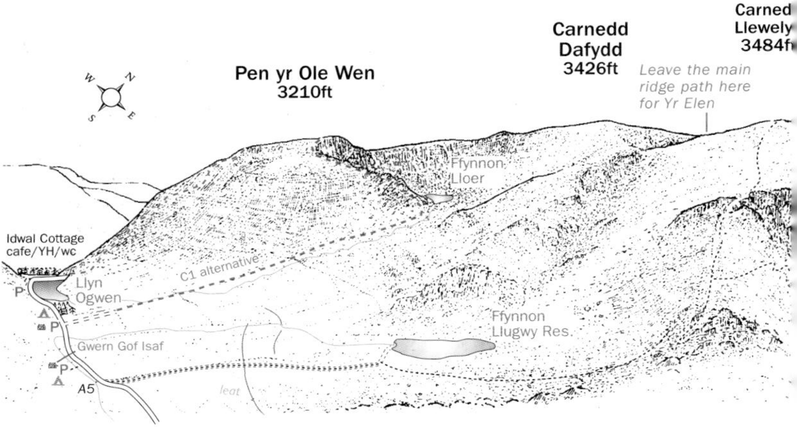

I wonder how many people owe a debt of thanks to their mysterious benefactor.

For the Welsh Three Thousander, passing the refuge hut should herald the start of a triumphant period, taking those last steps in the fading evening light to the summit of Foel-fras with success assured and the anticipation of a well cooked meal and pint.

The CARNEDDAU the route

Ogwen to Foel-fras

15km (9 miles) height gain: 1700m

Eclipsing Ogwen, the precipitous fortress of Pen yr Ole Wen mocks the aching limbs, which have just surrendered over six hundred metres on a descent from the Glyders. In the space of 1.5km, or just a mile, all of that will have to be regained. More people fail at this point than anywhere else on the walk; but take heart, for once you have cracked this one the succeeding lofty Carneddau ridges will offer an easy-paced finale all the way to Foel-fras. (Alternatively, Variant Route C1, on page 82, gets you up the 600m rather less unpleasantly.)

Go through the gap stile in the stone wall (SH 6488 6058) just beyond the road bridge over the **Afon Ogwen** (*water source*).

After clambering over a series of rock steps to a grassy terrace, a fairly prominent path climbs steeply to higher slopes, which are clad with heather and bilberry. This gives way to loose scree, which is an unrelenting slog, nevertheless made bearable by stunning views across Ogwen to Tryfan's North Ridge and Cwm Idwal.

Having been duped by a couple of false summits it is a relief to see the cairn and wind-shelter at the eastern edge of Pen yr Ole Wen's large stony summit plateau (SH655619). That's presuming you can and you're not unfortunate enough to be staring into the mist.

Foel Grach, looking back from the path to Carnedd Uchaf

Carneddau 2
Carnedd Dafydd – Carnedd Llewelyn

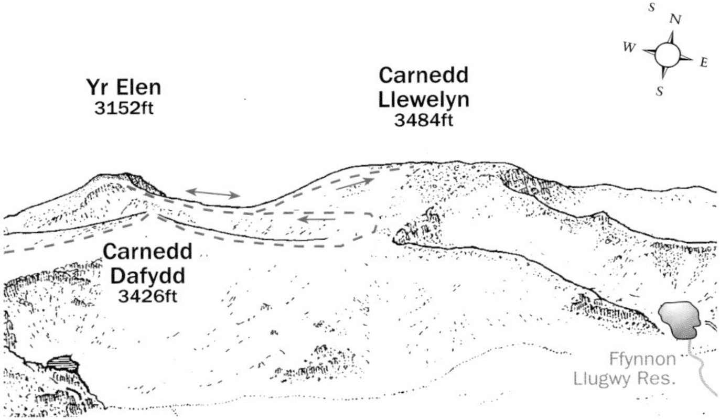

After some gradual walking across the large, grassy plateau to **Pen yr Ole Wen** summit, the path descends northwestwards to Bwlch yr Ole Wen. Here the delightful craggy arena of Cwm Lloer and its small tarn can be viewed to the right.

Follow the edge of the cwm on a broad ridge-top before climbing north-eastwards on an undulating ridge. There is a deceiving wind shelter set on elevated ground some ten minutes before reaching the summit of **Carnedd Dafydd** (SH 663630), which boasts another cairn and useful cross shaped wind-shelter.

One path descending from Carnedd Dafydd hugs the edge of Ysgolion Duon (the Black Ladders). An easier and faster course can be found on the grassy plateau just down to the right of the ridge.

Carnedd Llewelyn, though highest of the Carneddau, is uninteresting from this vantage. Its massif now lies ahead, but the Welsh 3000s route will first visit the shapely peak of Yr Elen. This is done by contouring Llewelyn's southern slopes. There are the beginnings of a path which soon die out. If you get it right you will pass a small spring (*water source*). The spring can usually be heard before it is seen, but it can dry up in the hot

Carneddau 3
Carnedd Llewelyn to Foel-fras

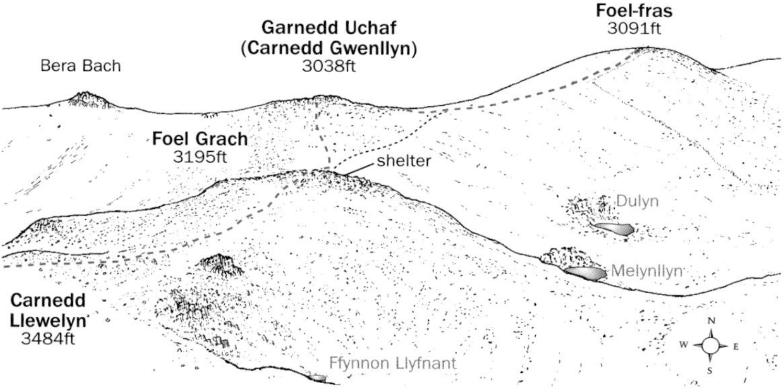

months so don't rely on it. Drop slightly to the col above Cwm Caseg, for the short but pleasantly serrated rocky ridgeline to **Yr Elen** (SH 673650). Being off the main ridge, this superb little peak is usually quiet and for the Welsh 3000's walker, an awkward detour.

Carnedd Llewelyn is now every bit a mountain, its rocky facade soaring above the shady depths of Cwm Caseg, whose diminutive tarn looks an idyllic wild campsite. After returning to the col a good path at the edge of the cwm climbs back onto **Carnedd Llewelyn**. The path veers to the right to attain the huge cairn and wind-shelter in the midst of Llewelyn's vast, stone-scattered, grassy summit plateau (SH 683643). Views have widened to encompass stretches of the North Wales coastline and the quilted emerald fields of the Conwy Valley, which lie beyond the sprawling grassy hills of the northern Carneddau. The final stages of our route to our last three mountains can be seen clearly from here. The ridges between Carnedd Llewelyn and Foel-fras are wide and have been improved with new stony paths.

From Llewelyn summit a cairned path descends roughly to north-northeast before a slight rise to the bouldered summit of

Looking back from Carnedd Uchaf to Carnedd Llewelyn (left) and Yr Elen

Foel Grach. Slightly to the north of the summit, camouflaged beneath crags, is the Refuge Shelter, much maligned by some who feel it is alien to the wildness of the mountain environment. This view would almost certainly not be shared by the travellers who have gratefully stumbled across it in adverse conditions. Personally I would be sad to see it go. To find the shelter from the summit, head north-east for 40 metres to the base of the rocky summit knoll. The hut is at the lowest rocks.

From Foel Grach follow the stone markers embedded in the grass and an obvious wide path northwards. Before the col, a faint path can be seen heading to the right, but this bypasses the next required summit. So keep straight ahead through the col, to the rock infused top of **Carnedd Uchaf**, the newest three thousander after re-surveying. The summit

The shelter hut innediately to north of the summit of Carnedd Uchaf

rockpile is west of the path (SH 6865 6689). Clamber over the rocky mound looking for the highest point, but you won't find any clues.

Now head off northeast across stony ground in search of the main path. This was once indistinct, but significant improvements have been made to it across the col to Foel-fras. After passing a marker stone at the head of the Afon Goch, the path becomes less stony and more peaty. The climb is gradual and sympathetic to the 3000s walker. As we get near the journey's end a fence is located and a stone ridge-wall accompanies us to **Foel-fras** trig point (SH 6964 6818). Somehow the dull top seems an unfitting climax to such a classic walk. However, there are fine views of the Welsh coastline and Conwy estuary, and the solitude of this northern outpost allows quiet contemplation of the day's triumphs.

Arriving at Foel-fras at the end of a long day over the Welsh 3000s

Getting off Foel-fras

Although we have completed our task, it is at least 6km (four miles) to that celebratory drink and a hearty meal.

If it comes to a final descent in the dark, the northward route off Foel-fras to Bwlch y Ddeufaen is the best one, as its slopes are gentle and there is a guiding fence or wall throughout.

Path below Llyn Anafon (Route 4 off Foel-fras)

For those with friends to pick them up by car:

1 to Bwlch y Ddeufaen (SH721716)

6km (4 miles)

Continue along the ridge (aided by ridge fence) descending to the boggy col between Foel-fras and Drum (pronounced Drim). The path is quite obvious as it climbs over Drum, Carnedd y Ddelw and Drosgl to reach the Roman Road. Turn right to a car park at the terminus of the motor road 800 metres (half a mile) distant. The standing stones at the roadside (SH 7152 7177) attract visitors from afar.

2 to lane above Llanbedr-y-cennin (SH744694)

6km (4 miles)

Steeper and less straightforward than Option 1.

From Foel-fras continue northeast down the ridge for 1km to an intersection of fences (SH 704685). Descend beside the fence southeast. The slope eases, and in 400 metres you meet a right of way, which should be followed north-east beneath Pen y Castell and Penygadair to the road.

Another 2km of road walking gets you to Tal-y-Bont for a pub and frequent buses to Conwy or Betwys-y-Coed.

For the self reliant:

3 to Abergwyngregyn (Aber) by the Roman Road

12km (7 1/2 miles)

A much longer walk. Follow the ridge and fence northeast to **Drum** where a rough vehicle track leads to the old Roman Road (SH693722). Turn left (west) along the old road, which becomes surfaced and follows the wooded lower valley of the Anafon to **Bont Newydd** before continuing to the village of Aber.

Descent to Llyn Anafon (Foel-fras exit route 4)

(Coastal bus service, or yet more walking, along coastal path, to Llanfairfechan railway station.)

4 to Abergwyngregyn (Aber) by Llyn Anafon

10km (6 miles)

The pleasant but initially rough way to Aber – requires daylight.

Follow the ridge and fence down northeast to the col between Foel-fras and Drum. A stone marker shows the way north-northwest towards **Llyn Anafon**. A steep and occasionally spongy path keeps to the right of the stream heading to the east side of the lake. From the right-hand end of the dam wall, steps lead down to a green lane. The path is followed for about 4.5km (3 miles). With pylons ahead, drop sharply left to a gate into a car park.

The lane beyond leads past another car park at **Bont Newydd** before continuing to Aber.

5 to Rowen Youth Hostel (SH747721)

8 km (5 miles)

Follow Option 1 by Bwlch y Ddeufaen. Continue down past the car park for 1.2km and take the left fork in the lanes. At Rowen there is a telephone box, a youth hostel, a B&B and the Ty Gwyn Hotel.

6 to Dulyn bothy (SH705664) and Cwm Eigiau car park (SH732663)

3km to bothy, 5km to car park

The shortest way off, but rough and steep. The bothy has no facilities.

Head south down a wall and then fence to the fence corner 500 metres from the summit. Cross a ladder stile and head down beside the fence, which becomes a wall lower down.

There's steep ground to descend, before you meet a track at the valley floor. Turn right for the bothy, below the track on the left in 800 metres; or cross the valley floor to a track opposite, and turn left to the car park.

For those linking the walk's two ends by Sherpa bus

7 to Gerlan / Bethesda

9km (5 1/2 miles)

Retrace steps back towards Carnedd Uchaf. Before reaching its summit, take the path which threads between this and Yr Aryg. A descent is then made on grassy slopes into Cwm Caseg, to reach a well-marked path that leads west to the head of a lane (SH 6388 6650). The lane passes through the colourful houses of Gerlan to reach Bethesda (Pesda locally, a large slate mining town famous for its slags).

The 3000s: route variations

The S2 Variant from Crib Goch to Llyn Glas

Variation S1 From Pen y Pass via Crib Goch

See map on page 54

Although not accepted for record purposes, this route is probably the fastest of all. The descent off Snowdon, though, is very steep, and there have been disputes over access at the foot of the slope.

From Pen y Pass follow the Snowdon Horseshoe route (Section 2) to **Crib Goch**, **Carnedd Ugain** and **Yr Wyddfa**.

The **Llanberis Path** (see Section 1) is used initially on the descent but it is abandoned by the railway bridge near Clogwyn Station (SH608561) for a precipitous and spectacular descent into **Cwm Glas Bach**. The route rakes left below the impressive cliffs of Llechog, then drops down a scree gully to a stream (*water source*). Here it deviates left to avoid rock ledges above the water's edge. The path becomes sketchy as it twists round crags and down very steep and sometimes slippery grassy slopes with a rocky spur to the left.

After going through a gap in a drystone wall (SH611570), head north-eastwards for some sheepfolds before veering left and passing the front of the Cwm Glas Bach Cottage, avoiding the house. Here an access lane leads to a bridge spanning over Afon Nant Peris. *Please note that the lane is a negotiated courtesy route to the access area beneath Carnedd Ugain: be considerate.* Turn left and continue via **Nant Peris** to the Glyderau.

Variation S2 Crib Goch descent via Bwlch Goch

See map on page 54

This variation can be marginally faster than the descent via Crib goch's North Ridge. It was used by Colin Donnelly in his record run of 1988.

From Crib Goch summit, retrace steps past the Pinnacles to **Bwlch Goch**, the pass between Crib Goch and Carnedd Ugain. The key to the route is to descend the steep, scree-strewn flanks northwards into **Cwm Uchaf**. (From Bwlch Goch, many try to contour the easier slopes to the left beneath Clogwyn y Person, but consequently find themselves with crags and cliffs to negotiate.) From the marshy bowl of Cwm Uchaf continue along the eastern banks of the stream (*water source*) that drains its tiny pools. The path, which varies between faint and non-existent, threads through crags and bluffs down into **Cwm Glas Mawr**, where you ford the stream. After traversing marshy grasslands and fording two more streams (SH618562 and SH617563), the route joins a well-defined stony path. This descends close to the western banks of the main stream, passing the cottage of **Blaen-y-nant** before recrossing the stream via a wooden footbridge. After crossing another bridge, this time over the Afon Nant Peris, the road is met and followed to the left into Nant Peris.

N.B: It is possible to vary the route from Cwm Uchaf by heading northwest over grassy flanks to **Llyn Glas** (*water source*), a beautiful tarn set beneath the imposing cliffs of Clogwyn y Person. The eastern banks of the tarn are traced before turning right opposite its island. Soon after descending stony flanks a

Tryfan from the east, showing the line of Heather Terrace below the crags

footpath becomes evident. It descends bouldery slopes close to the western banks of a stream (SH619560) before joining the previously mentioned route beneath the cliffs in the marshy environs of **Cwm Glas Mawr**.

Variation G1 off Tryfan by Bwlch Tryfan

See map on page 62

There are various routes off Tryfan, each with its own combination of speed, steepness and scenery. The quickest is described in the main text above. The slowest – for experienced mountaineers only – would be to scramble down Glyder Fach's Bristly Ridge then down Tryfan's spiky North Ridge; but both are better in ascent than descent, and so more suitable to a north to south traverse (see Section 5).

This Variant G1 is less eroded and more comfortable than the quicker route of the main text. Retrace steps from the summit of Tryfan to **Bwlch Tryfan** and then take the path down right (northwest) to **Llyn Bochlwyd** (also known as Lake Australia), one of the range's many delightful tarns. The path has been repaired in recent years and leads directly to Idwal Cottage.

Variation G2 off Tryfan by Heather Terrace

See map on page 62

This is a slower, but very romantic and interesting, route down Tryfan. It is rocky, but without actual scrambling. It sets you up nicely for Variation C1, the East Ridge of Pen yr Ole Wen, following.

Return to the col north of Far South Peak. A short wall runs across this col. Cross its ladder stile. Beyond, a stony open gully descends east-southeast. You can descend this for 200 metres, then contour left on a small path past a cairn; but it's nicer is to descend east, on a scrambly path just above and to left of the open gully, to reach the same small path.

Either way the path now slants down to the left, northeast. It is well used and passes down the slanting **Heather Terrace** immediately below all the rock climbs of Tryfan's East Face. Beyond the crags the path continues slanting down in the same direction. As it approaches the foot of the slope it slants down across a scree slope, then around a corner with a perched block, to reach the foot of Tryfan's North Ridge.

At this spot (SH 6674 5998) is the top of a deep little gully descending northeast. Go down the gully, which has stone steps in it. A path runs down and to the right, with a fence above on the right. A steep stony path turns off directly downhill, to reach a metal kissing gate at the main road, just where a bridleway track joins from Gwern Gof Uchaf.

Variation G3 off Tryfan to Llyn Ogwen Foot

See map on page 62 and picture page 178

This steep and unpleasant route down Tryfan is the fastest for runners, competent in descent, who then continue by C1, the East Ridge of Pen yr Ole Wen, following. For such strong descenders it gives a less strenuous ascent of the Pen and saves a minute or two.

Descending the steep south ridge of Pen yr Ole Wen. Variant C1 (by the east ridge) lets you avoid this, with a considerable gain in comfort and only a very slight loss of time.

Opposite: the scrambly bit of Pen yr Ole Wen's east ridge

Follow the main West Gully route down its steep rocky path to the 750m contour. Now bear right down steep, stony, slopes along the foot of Tryfan's western crags, to the car park near Llyn Ogwen foot. See picture on page 178.

Variation C1 Pen Yr Ole Wen via its East Ridge

See map on page 68

Although not quite as quick as the south ridge route, this delightful alternative is definitely for the connoisseur, offering fine views over Ffynnon Lloer.

The route begins on the A5 road at the track end 300 metres east of Llyn Ogwen (SH668605, small roadside pull-in). A public footpath sign points northwards to a gravel track that dissects a small fir plantation and passes **Glan Dena**, the Midland Mountaineers Association's cottage. Just before reaching a farm, the track is abandoned for a path to the right, which follows a wall northwards to a ladder stile. The stile is scaled and an intermittent path strikes northwards uphill for 300 metres to cross the **Afon Lloer** (*water source*) and run up beside it over ground which can be boggy after heavy rain. The gradient steepens on approaching the intake wall (at the border of pastureland and mountainside) which is scaled by a stile (SH667617) beside a gate.

An indistinct path (east-northeast) now leads to the higher ground of the east ridge. A large crag appears to bar the way. Closer examination reveals a gully and an easy scramble up it gains the ridge. Here a delightful path climbs over heather and crag with a sudden view into the exquisite Cwm Lloer and its gem of a tarn. Views of the Glyders are enlivened by the wedge of Tryfan, Glyder Fawr, and the Devil's Kitchen.

In the final stages the stony path hugs the edge of the cwm on the right, before leading westwards to **Pen yr Ole Wen's** summit cairn. Here it meets the main route to Carnedd Dafydd.

4

Fifteen Wet Welsh Mountains

by Ronald Turnbull

The Welsh 3000s

Fifteen Wet Welsh Mountains

by Ronald Turnbull

Mathematics has no place in the mountains. There's something rather sad about counting down to some arbitrary fixed line and doing those tops while ignoring all others. True: except when the mountains are Welsh ones, and the line is at 3000 feet.

Indeed, we are forced to the conclusion that some ancient Egyptian surveyor was truly inspired. Somehow, his ascents of the Great Pyramid gave him mystic foreknowledge of the needs of Welsh walkers 5000 years in the future. If, before defining for us the length of the foot, that ancient surveyor hadn't remembered to cut his toenails, this Welsh walk would not have included Tryfan. You only need to add one hundredth of an inch to the foot to exclude Tryfan, probably the single most essential summit of the walk.

The Great Pyramid has a clear 144m of drop all round. Apply this concept to the Welsh Three-thousands and you'll only get six summits. Six is not enough. You can argue endlessly as to whether Crib Goch is a mountain, or Glyder Fach. Contrariwise, the hummock of Castell y Gwynt has been considered to qualify under the fifty-foot drop rule and the hummock of Clogwyn y Person hasn't. And what about Carnedd Uchaf, which sneaked up past the line one day in 1983 when the Ordnance Survey weren't looking? Such argument is enjoyable enough. It is, however, less enjoyable than a walk across Snowdonia that includes Crib Goch and Glyder Fach, and doesn't bother with Clogwyn y Person.

For slice it how you will, the walk across the fifteen Welsh Three-thousands is one of the best single-day mountain walks anywhere. (And the walk across the sixteen of them, supposing you think there are sixteen, is every bit as excellent.) It's a walk

Previous page: Aber Falls

sunset over the Glyder plateau

that's hard - very hard - but not impossible. It has wide and interesting views. Many of these views are over the edges of big cliffs. It has three quite different mountain ranges; grassy Carneddau, stony Glyders, and steep rocky Snowdon. It has the best ridge-scramble south of Scotland.

And it has 29 demanding miles (45 rough kilometres) and 3900 steep metres of ascent.

Why, then, did I try to make this most interesting of walks even more interesting? Why did I start at the sea instead of that draughty but convenient road below Foel-fras? Why plan on adding Tryfan's North Ridge and Glyder's Bristly one to the high delights of Crib Goch? And why, given one of the best walks anywhere, attempt to not walk but run the thing in a time not exceeding 8 hrs and 25 minutes?

For the 8 hrs and 25 minutes there is actually an explanation. 59 years before, Thomas Firbank had crossed these hills in 8 hrs 25. It was, in its time, a record-breaking run. It was an outrageous, even a controversial run - his two companions apologised afterwards, in the pages of the Climbers' Club Magazine. And he wrote about it, in a book called *I Bought a Mountain*, in a way that makes anyone with a pair of boots want to put them on, take them off again, and place them thoughtfully on the kitchen scales...

And the rest of it? Well, the technicalities can be found in the works of the Greek philosopher Aristotle, particularly those bits where he deals with the construction of Tragic Drama. But, to set the thing down briefly on the corner of a map, there's HUBRIS, when you think it'd be interesting do some extra bits like maybe Y Lliwedd. And there's NEMESIS, when the gods say: "Interesting? We'll give him interesting. We'll give him some interesting weather, ho ho!"

So I started from Aber, and yes, it was interesting, with the grey mudflats at dawn, and the dripping oakwood, and the path that slithers across wet rocks at the top of the waterfall, and the secret stream valley above. But up on Foel-fras it was snowing. And the path along the Carneddau is broad and muddy until you get to where you'd rather like there to be a path, and there it disappears into a heap of wet boulders. I hurried along the Carneddau, slightly despising the muddy path for thinking itself the best long walk in Britain, and sneering at the wet boulders: so you think you're going to twist my ankles, me in my little blue running shoes? I tell you, the boulders of Ben Nevis ripped the little blue shoes right off my feet! But then the mists heaved apart, and peering into the clouded depths as into a crystal ball I beheld my immediate future. For me the future held black rocks, and high steep slopes, and Tryfan. And before that, a sharp rocky ridge to Yr Elen that was so nice I was going to do it twice.

Why suffer unnecessarily? I came off Pen yr Ole Wen by the East Ridge, which is the nice way, the fairly gentle way, the way with the short gully scramble and the grassy slopes to the A5. It's also the way with the view of Tryfan. The ideal of mountain

Carnedd Uchaf and Foel-fras

form is the Matterhorn as seen from Zermatt; but from 500m on the Afon Lloer, Tryfan actually looks sharper than the Matterhorn, and thus not altogether convincing.

Cloud ripped away from the crest, just as it does on the Matterhorn. Up there, rain would be dripping sideways across grey stones, and a line of historic footholds leads across the top of a horrifying drop.

On the Matterhorn, they let you wear a rope... And I'd had a warning from a Competent Hillwalker, a member of the Mountain Rescue. The rocks of Tryfan are treacherously greasy when wet. No matter that this seems unlikely, the total cleanliness of Tryfan's rocks being assured by an atmosphere that's much the same as the inside of a car-wash machine. No matter that I'd been there before, in just such treacherous weather, and trodden the wide but windswept footholds, stepped delicately across the tops of the famous rock climbs. Wise Old Men of the Mountains have a curiously demoralising effect on hillrunners out all alone at silly times of the year.

And really, Heather Terrace is such an interesting way up Tryfan, even if it isn't quite so interesting as the North Ridge. I patted the top of the summit block, and the sun popped out briefly, making Tryfan gleam like a crocodile emerging from the grey-green Limpopo River. Then down Tryfan, boulder by boulder, like a kitten on a staircase. I met a group of women coming up. "Oh – is there anybody else up there?"

If there had been, they'd blown away. But why did they seek solitude in – of all places – busy Tryfan? Suspiciously, I counted. They were indeed thirteen. Clearly they planned, once up, to fling aside their dripping Gore-tex and perform unspeakable rituals around the summit stones.

Wet weather travel fogs the brain as well as the hilltops. It was I – I with my fifteen three-thousanders in wet March – who was performing the unspeakable ritual.

After deciding not to do the North Ridge, it doesn't take much thinking to decide not to do the Bristly one either. I inched belly-down across Glyder Fach's summit boulder, up into the gale and down again, and traversed the Castell y Gwynt which jolly well deserves to be a Welsh Three-thousander. Its

Tryfan and Llyn Ogwen

fifty-one feet of drop consist of jammed vertical rock-splinters. Who wants to look like the Matterhorn when you can look like a hedgehog doing the high-jump? This Glyder Plateau doesn't take itself terribly seriously, and when you lose your compass, or your leg, down a hole between two boulders, the boulders concerned are amusingly shaped like Mae West's lips, or nutcrackers, or a bunch of bananas. The bigger Glyder has a great joke: you clamber up its summit rockpile and from its top you see, shadowy in the mist, a slightly higher summit rockpile 20 metres further on. The joke wears a little thin: there are seven summit rockpiles.

Cairns mark the line off Glyder Fawr and other cairns mark another line, and indeed any line you care to take has a cairn to comfort you. I used hillrunners' instinct – hillrunners like to do things quickly, and hillrunners' instinct is the quick way to get lost. When I finally got out the map, I found that there were only five mountains left. And the next two were simple ridge-running, a path stretched like a guy rope across the high green tent of the western Glyders. The cloud lifted a little, and elegant Snowdonian shapes stood one behind the other across the Llanberis valley: Eilio and Y Garn, Cynghorion and distant Hebog.

At the final Glyder I met a Youth Behavioural Worker, relaxing after a tough 24-hr shift by walking up Elidir Fawr very fast. He seemed amused by my uncool concern to find the higher cairn, offered to certify my presence on the very summit. Great! Would he like to come along and certify Crib Goch and Snowdon as well? Elidir Fawr looks steep on the map but in fact it's fast and grassy, and at Nant Peris there were still almost two hours left for beating Thomas Firbank in, and the cloud had lifted a little so maybe the rock was going to be nice and dry along those alarming Pinnacles. Anyway, I already did those alarming Pinnacles, I was thirteen at the time and my little sister came too, in her flip-flops. So the Pinnacles wouldn't be a problem.

Indeed the cloud had lifted, but it was just the Gods peering under the grey lid to see how their hubristic soup was bubbling.

If Glaslyn is the heart of Snowdonia (and it is), Llanberis Pass is Snowdonia's buttock cleavage. It's tight and it's black and at 100m above sea level it's all mountain. On either side of the road, rock slopes rise vigorously to the 600m contour or to the cloud, whichever is lower. The flat bit at the bottom is entirely occupied by several huge boulders fallen from above.

There are eight main ways up Snowdon, but the way by Cwm Glas Mawr is something else again. The eight main ways comprise six airy ridgewalks, one airy ridge-scramble, and the deep-walled tarn of Glaslyn. Cwm Glas Mawr is a wrinkle in the north-eastern rockface, a place where the crags open apart to let the water out. The instructions are to go up to left of the left-hand waterfall, but I was having trouble with those waterfalls. The second from the left, for instance, set off down a high black overhang: but it was only half a waterfall, then the rest of it just blew away into the wind. The left-hand waterfall came down a serious rockface, but I went up for a look anyway. And it was all right. The rocks leant back, there were ledges and handholds, people went this way. And so what if the waterfall was blowing out sideways and splashing all over the ledges and handholds?

And so up a high green place on the side of Snowdon to Crib Goch's North Ridge. That ridge is sharp, and probably has exhilarating views eastwards; I stayed low, below the crest,

Crib Goch seen from Glyder Fawr, with the north ridge, shaded, sweeping down to the right. Y Lliwedd is behind, left.

below the wind. After a while things sharpened further, and steepened. The side of the ridge was rotten rock leading to a scree slot. The top of the ridge was firm; but the wind was enjoying itself up there, making loud noises across the jagged edge. The cloud was back down and it was raining. And maybe little sisters in flip-flops don't have any trouble on the Pinnacles, but I wasn't a little sister in flip-flops and I was getting unhappy. So I descended 200m, crossed below the Clogwyn y Person and above the two small tarns, and went up Carnedd Ugain by its untrodden North Ridge.

"Ho ho," went the Gods of the Mountain again. "Crossed the Carnedds and Glyders in 6 1/2 hours, got within 30m of Crib Goch with 32 minutes still on the clock, and didn't do the Welsh Threethousands! Is that a puny human, or what?"

Well certainly that's a puny human: Colin Donnelly's done the Welsh Threes in four hours twenty. But not doing Crib Goch means I can come back and do them all again next year, which'll be the anniversary of Firbank's 8hrs 25. And listen, Gods: I'm a hillrunner, I enjoyed doing the Carnedds and the Glyders in 6 1/2 hours. A bad person is still a person, and a slow hillrunner is still a hillrunner, and at Bwlch Glas to prove it I ran the final

100m up Snowdon. There's a handy hole in the top of the trig point where I can leave my bit of seaweed from Conwy Bay.

Glaslyn is where times and summits, if they ever mattered, don't any more. Trace the ridges around Glaslyn with the eye – better, with the feet – Crib Goch and Lliwedd and Gribin. Volcanic ash all carved by ice, those ridge lines wind themselves around the heart as they do around the lake of Glaslyn that's the heart of Snowdonia. The very boulders in the water are carved into the same sharp shapes. Dusk, and no camera, and no-one else around: this is one of many ways to see Glaslyn. It's nice running, too, along the reconstructed Miners Track. And as I emerge, blinking, into the lights of the car park, I've achieved something quite out of the ordinary.

I've crossed crowded Snowdon, from Llanberis roadside to Pen y Pass, without meeting anybody else at all.

Looking back up the Pig Track to Crib Goch, from above Pen y Pass

5
The Three Thousands north to south

On Bristly Ridge, Glyder Fach

The Threethousanders: Which Way?

There are two ways of doing – or trying to do – the 15 Welsh Peaks of 3000ft (915m). You can run them, trying to beat the famous Firbank time of 8 1/2 hours, or the Joss Naylor time of 4 hrs 45 mins, or, if you really think you're hard, the Colin Donnelly time of 4 hrs 19 mins 54 seconds. You'll start on Snowdon; you'll take an odd little backtrack off Crib Goch avoiding some very nice ridge but gaining almost two minutes; you'll eat jam sandwiches all the way up Pen yr Ole Wen and drink through a tube.

Or you can walk them, as a once-in-a-lifetime challenge, aiming simply to survive. Again you'll start on Snowdon; you'll take the grim scree route off Glyder Fach and an even grimmer one off Tryfan; and again you'll eat sandwiches all the way up Pen yr Ole Wen.

Either way you'll have a fine day out on one of Britain's very finest mountain ranges – and then another of Britain's very finest mountain ranges – and then yet a third of Britain's very finest mountain ranges. Snowdon, Glyder and Carnedd; rocky ridge, boulderfield, gentle grass and mighty crag: it's a full and satisfying day for any walker, or of course a very full 4 hrs 20 mins for Colin Donnelly.

But there's a third way – a way for those of us too slow for serious running, but vigorous enough not to be intimidated by 40km and 3000m of ascent (25 miles and 10,000ft). The Welsh Three Thousands, as usually attacked, have some sections that aren't totally delightful. The descent to Tryfan: the even worse descent after Tryfan: the very steep 600m climb up Pen yr Ole Wen. By turning the whole thing around and starting from a bivvy on Foel-fras, you achieve a Welsh Threes with added treat. The grassy slopes of Foel-fras offer bivvy sites far superior to the back wall of the Snowdon summit café. Dawn light flowing across the Carneddau; the ascent of Tryfan's exhilarating North Ridge; the ascent of equally exhilarating Bristly Ridge immediately afterwards; and the intrepid could even take in the Jammed Boulder Gully of Crib Goch. Then sunset all along Crib Goch and Crib y Ddysgl. As a finale – and given that you've already completed half of the Snowdon Horseshoe – you could end off over Y Lliwedd. Alternatively, a schedule timed to arrive 10 mins before the last train down Snowdon will add momentum to the entire trip.

Getting to Foel-fras

The fastest way to get to the summit of Foel-fras is to get someone to drive you to the end of the Bwlch y Ddeufaen road (SH721715). From the pass itself at the track top, take a grassy path to right of a wall up Drosgl's north-eastern ridge. The wall becomes a fence as you cross Drum and then a wall again up onto Foel-fras. The guiding wall and fence make this a reasonably easy route in the dark.

An alternative start is from a car park behind Aber. Your friendly driver can take you past Bont Newydd to the end of the lane (SH676715). Here a stony track is used to climb to Drum, turning right at the crossroads (SH693722) between Garreg Fawr and Foel-ganol. Or take the shorter track to Llyn Anafon, especially if you fancy a steep climb out to the col between Drum and Foel-fras.

Foel-fras can also be reached by its southeast slopes from the car park at Llyn Eigiau (SH732663) or from the bothy at Dulyn Reservoir (SH705664). Those using Sherpa bus to link the start with the end at Pen y Pass will approach from Bethesda. Best is east along Afon Caseg and through the gap between Carnedd Uchaf and Yr Aryg.

A ladder stile at Foel-fras summit leads across to grassy bivvy sites on what is usually the sheltered side of the wall.

ahead to Yr Elen, from Carnedd Uchaf

The Route: Carneddau

From **Foel-fras** trig point follow the wall downhill. Where it becomes fence, the path bends away slightly right, and is partly paved through the col. The clear path runs up **Carnedd Uchaf** to its stony summit area, with the summit rockpile 20 metres to the right of where the path arrives.

Cross stony ground southwards until the path reforms. It is wide and clear through the col and up to the shelter on **Foel Grach** at the foot of its rocky summit knoll. (To find the shelter from the summit, head north-east for 40 metres to the base of the rocky summit knoll. The hut is at the lowest rocks.)

The ground around the sprawling cairn is stony and pathless. Head south towards the next col, with a path joining from the right and leading up the stony slope of **Carnedd Llewelyn**. A small cairn marks the arrival at the plateau edge, with a larger one after 100 metres at the true summit, and a shelter cairn 30 metres beyond.

From the summit cairn head north-west across the summit plateau to blocky outcrops at its corner. A small path runs down the ridge to a col, and up a pleasantly narrow ridge to **Yr Elen**. There are three summits, with the middle one being highest.

Return down the nice pathed ridge to the col. After a few steps, a scree path forks off right, climbing slightly around the flank of Llewelyn. It crosses the first (southwest-pointing) spur just above its steeper section. From here there's no clear path. Contour round, crossing two small but useful streams (*water source*), to reach the col Bwlch Cyfryw-drum. Here join a ridge path coming down from Llewelyn.

After a short rise, the path joins a crossing ridge. The ridge crest is stony and rocky, with an easier path on grass 20 metres down on the left. The ridge crest widens, with a wide path, to the summit of **Carnedd Dafydd**. The ridge path leads on southwest to **Pen yr Ole Wen**.

There's a small summit cairn, with a much larger shelter cairn 100 metres away down the southwest ridge – which ridge we don't want to take. Instead bear left at the summit cairn to follow a well-used path down the east ridge. Scramble down an easy groove on the way down, before the path reaches the **Afon Lloer** stream (*water*). A wall below is crossed with a ladder stile. The path continues down through bracken to right of the stream, marked by occasional yellow topped poles. Above buildings turn left to a ladder stile over a wall. Then turn right down a pitched path to join a gravel access track. It leads out through a gate and a small wood to **Glan Dena**, and the A5 east of Llyn Ogwen. There's a small parking pull-off.

The Route: The Glyderau

From the **Glan Dena** track end (SH668605) cross 20 metres right, to a metal kissing gate at a footpath signpost (immediately to right of a track leading towards Gwern Gof Uchaf). A small rough path slants up left, then directly uphill, where it is mistakable for a stream. Where a fence is seen above on the left, slant up right into a scree gully. Stone steps, usually partly scree-covered, have been built inside the narrow gully. It emerges on the crest of Tryfan's north ridge.

Up Tryfan by Heather Terrace

Heather Terrace involves no real scrambling, but is still an interesting and scenic way up Tryfan. As an ascent route it is probably just as quick as the more usual walkers' route by Tryfan's western slopes and Llyn Bochlwyd. Its ruggedness, though, would make it a slow choice as a descent.

Immediately at the top of the narrow gully with the steps inside, turn left on a small path. Slant uphill and left around a corner with a perched block, to a scree run that drops to the left. The path slants up across this, becoming clear at the further side.

The path slants gradually up Tryfan's eastern flank, passing along the base of all the climbing crags (small streams, water supply*). Eventually a scree-filled hollow is just ahead: it comes down from Tryfan's Far South Col. Either keep ahead past a cairn to the scree, and head up it, to the right, for 200 metres to the col; or else turn up alongside the scree hollow on zigzag ledges and short scrambles. Either way, reach the* ***Far South Col****, which has a wall across it with a single ladder stile, and is immediately north of Far South Peak.*

A direct line up right for the summit involves some good but rather steep scrambling. Instead, contour forward and head around to left of the steep scrambling, to find a worn path heading uphill. There's some bouldery clambering before you reach ***Tryfan*** *summit with its two upstanding rocks.*

posed scrambling on the direct route up the final per of Tryfan's North Ridge – the easier line is tured on the next page.

On the easier route that outflanks Tryfan's final tower

Up Tryfan's North Ridge

Once you emerge from the narrow gully with steps in, Tryfan's north ridge is a wide buttress with many paths and optional scrambly bits. Simply head up it, enjoying the scrambling or where necessary finding an easier way around on one of the paths.

At roughly half-height, the ridgeline narrows at a quartz terrace. Here head right for 20 metres to find **the Cannon**, a photogenic projecting rock which is not visible from the main upward path. 100 metres above, the ridge narrows onto a grassy sloping terrace.

From the top of the terrace rises the rock-tower that's the real scrambling bit.

You could go straight up this on good, well-used holds, but quite steep and exposed (Grade 2). Two thirds of the way up the tower, a ledge round to the right gives promise of an easier continuation, but straight up is ok.

More easily, from the cairn at the base of this final tower (SH 6647 5960), descend left through a rock gap onto a path that heads out around the eastern face. As the path slants slightly uphill, you can scramble up leftwards on easy rocks above it. Or remain on the path as it reaches a gully on the eastern face (SH 6647 5954). (The path continues beyond the gully, but ignore that.)

The first step up this gully is an awkward chockstone boulder. Avoid this by not entering the gully, but scrambling a few metres beside it (on its right) to enter it above the chockstone. Head up the gully to its top, bridged by a jammed boulder. Above this, arrive at the notch in the main ridgeline above the steep tower (SH 6644 5954).

Turn left to scramble the easier-angled crest above towards Tryfan's **North Top**. This can be scrambled by a gully right of centre, or outflanked on the right. Cross a small col (North Col) to **Tryfan's** main summit with its upstanding stones Adam and Eve.

A direct line over Tryfan's South Top and Far South Top for Bwlch Tryfan would involve some quite steep down-scrambling on good rock. So the easiest line down does not follow that crest line ahead, but slants down rather to its right (west). It is a worn, cairned path, with occasional moments of boulder-clambering but no real scrambling. The worn path passes just below (to right of) the first, very shallow col before South Top. Now paths slant down, rather to right of the crest, to pass below and to the right of the small Far South Col (which has a wall across, and a ladder stile, and is where the path up from Heather Terrace arrived). Don't visit this col, but head down away from the wall, on Tryfan's west flank, still on stony paths with occasional short boulder-scrambles. Once you're below the rocky top section, the path leads round left into **Bwlch Tryfan**.

A wall crosses the pass, with two ladder stiles. Ignore those, staying to right (west) of the wall. As the ground rises ahead, the path heads away from the wall, passing to right of a broken outcrop (itself to right of the wall) to reach the foot of **Bristly Ridge**.

Above, the steep main crag is split by a gully with a blocking boulder near its foot. Go up in this gully (or on broken rocks to the right to avoid the initial scree). Get onto the boulder using large helpful holds, and climb the gully above, which gets

scramblers off-route while descending Bristly Ridge. The easier route is by the gully groove seen to left of the pinnacle.

quite steep and exposed, and indeed is the hardest bit of the scramble.

Paths lead up the broad crest above – the left-hand edge has sudden steep drops that are very dramatic. The crest narrows, forcing you onto the crest as it forms a small tower. This is the Bristly Bit! Cross the tower, heading down on the right-hand (west) side then passing a few steps to the left, into the gap behind it. Beyond this gap rises an intimidating pinnacle. Go left, through the gap, slanting up around the base of this second pinnacle into the groove on its left. The groove is gently-angled with good holds, and leads onto the crest above and behind the pinnacle.

The crest is now easy, finally dipping slightly to let you step off onto the stony plateau of **Glyder Fach**. Turn right along the plateau edge, passing to right of the poised boulder called the Cantilever, to the summit rockpile. It is climbed most easily from its far side. Get down off it and continue south-west towards the next spiky hedgehog, **Castell y Gwynt**.

From the slight col just before Castell y Gwynt, a path passes down to left, bending right below the rocky tower. It's just as quick, and more fun, to scramble straight across. The cairned path continues just below and left of the pass Bwlch y Ddwy Glyder, and across the stony plateau of Glyder Fawr. Various rockpiles are ahead; the most westerly has two flakes that you can pass between and is **Glyder Fawr's** true summit.

Head left (just south of west) for about 50 metres to find a path with sprawling cairns. It runs northwest down gentle stoneslopes, with many cairns. With Llyn y Cwn (the Dog Lake) visible below, bend to the right down a steep scree path, then bear right down a slanting stony gully, to pass to right of **Llyn y Cwn**.

Ahead, two clear paths run up Y Garn, each crossing a ladder stile above the slope foot; above its stile, the smaller right hand path gives some views over the edge on the right.

Head down from **Y Garn** on a path beside the drops on the right. At the col below, take a contouring path ahead across the west slope of Foel-goch. It crosses a ladder stile, and swings round into the col before Mynydd Perfedd. The path contours on around the south slope of Mynydd Perfedd and onto the slope of Elidir Fawr. At a fork, take the higher path to gain the ridgeline just above. A nice rocky ridge, or path on the flank down left, leads to the stony summit of **Elidir Fawr**.

On the Glyder ridgeline west of Y Garn

Descending Elidir Fawr, with Crib Goch (left) and Carnedd Ugain looming ahead. It's late in the day, but this threethousander will eventually reach Yr Wyddfa just before midnight.

Descend the stony south slope, awkwardly, for 20 metres, to find a rough path. This slants down to the right (south) across the face below, soon leaving stones for grass, and passes through two gaps in erosion-control fences. Below the second of these, the path slants down right, to a ladder stile. Slant on down to a footbridge not visible from above (SH608596). On the wide green path beyond it, turn down right, above a stream with many small waterfalls. The path bends away from the stream and descends in a zig-zag, then fades in a field. Pass to right of a stone barn to join a tarred track at a gate with a ladder stile.

Head down the lane to a junction, and turn right on a track to right of the river, to join the A4086 beside its bridge in **Nant Peris**.

In lower Cwm Glas Mor. The scrambly path goes up just to left of the waterfall. Crib Goch is on the skyline far above. (Photo: John Gillham)

The Route: Snowdon

Turn left on the A4086 through **Nant Peris**. After 50 metres pass the Vaynol Arms, then follow the walled road towards Llanberis Pass. After 2km (1 1/2 miles) or so, a bridge on the right is marked '**Blaen Nant**' to house and camp site.

Cross the wooden bridge to go up a path to right of a stream. After passing through a wall gap, head left across the stream, to join a sidestream with a wall going up alongside it on the far (left-hand) side.

The wall and stream lead up into a rock amphitheatre. A steep blackened rockwall ahead has a waterfall coming down (if wet) or half-way down (if wet and very windy). 50 metres left of this is a small waterfall stream. Immediately to left of this stream a path goes up in zig-zags with occasional short rock steps.

From the stream top, you can see up to the north ridge of Crib Goch, whose cone-shaped end is visible in the notch far above. Head directly uphill to the base of that scree cone.

The North Ridge of Crib Goch

Small paths slant up leftwards to the apex of the scree, and the beginning of the **North Ridge**. A gently-rising crest of rather poor reddish rock leads on and up. To start with there's a scree path on the right. This is loose, so take to the crest itself as it sharpens and steepens. The final steep rise can be taken direct; or can be avoided by following a ledge for 10 metres to the left and climbing a small corner, to reach Crib Goch's small **north summit**.

Turn right along the rocky crest, whose many holds are clean and much-trodden. The easiest way is to use footholds a little way down on the left (Glaslyn) side, using the crest itself for handhold. Scree paths further down left appear easier but are less safe.

The ridge crosses **Crib Goch**'s main summit, dips, then rises in two **pinnacles**. Pass around these to the left on scree shelves. Ahead is a gap with a further pinnacle beyond.

Happy scramblers will pass to the right, through the gap, onto the northern face. Here a narrow ramp passes up the flank of the pinnacle to its top – this is exposed, but holds are good, and it's not steep. Cross the pinnacle to descend rather to left of its crest (Glaslyn side) to the grassy col **Bwlch Goch**.
To avoid the final pinnacle: head down left in a gully of spiky holds for 30m vertical. Don't go too far down, as scree below the turnoff point looks walked-on but has simply slid down. Look out for a well-trodden ledge heading out right (for someone looking downhill), across the base of the final pinnacle, then heading up to the crest behind it. A steep path now leads down bare rock to the levelling at **Bwlch Goch**.

A path leads along **Bwlch Goch's** fairly narrow and rocky crest, then runs along just down left of the crest (or there's a smaller path weaving among the crestline rocks). After 200 metres the main path rejoins the ridge crest. Ahead, that crest is rockier and slightly steeper. Here a tempting and well-used path contours off left avoiding the obstacle – but this deposits you into the middle of a large nasty hillside of scree and outcrop. So don't!

Instead head straight up the crest, on easy scrambling, either slightly to right of the crest line, or straight up it. After another levelling, a steeper tower can start with a short steep wall, with good holds: or take easier lines round to the left. Continue up the left flank, on good scrambling with large holds, to the crest behind the tower. This is blocky-rocky, as Crib Goch was, but this time the way is just on the right-hand (Llanberis Pass) side of the crest, or on a path immediately below.

The ridge becomes stony, with a sprawling cairn almost filling a small col. Continuing along the crest, the path avoids some rocky obstructions, although they can be enjoyably scrambled. A steeper step is taken by a 10m groove on the right, with the trig on **Carnedd Uchaf** not far beyond.

A wide stony path leads down to the Pigtop Pillar in the col **Bwlch Glas** where the Pig Track arrives from down on the left.

A wide path continues ahead to left of the railway. Scenic (but possibly windy) bivvy sites are on the grass between this path and the brink above. Alternative bivvies, depending on wind direction, are 10 metres down the south-east ridge from **Yr Wyddfa's** summit cairn.

Descending from Snowdon

The Llanberis route is wide and easy to follow by moonlight or torchlight, and its western orientation holds the last of the daylight. It is, however, distressingly long. A night-time descent of the Pig Track is dark and dramatic, but does need care to avoid going wrong on the zig-zags. Both these descents are described in Section 1.

The romantic alternative, especially after a summit bivvy, is to continue around the Snowdon Horseshoe. After all, you've done half of it already, and including Y Lliwedd adds less than an hour to the descent time. See 'Snowdon Horseshoe Anticlockwise' in Section 2.

On Y Lliwedd, at dawn, after a Snowdon summit bivvy

6

The Welsh 1000 Metre Peaks

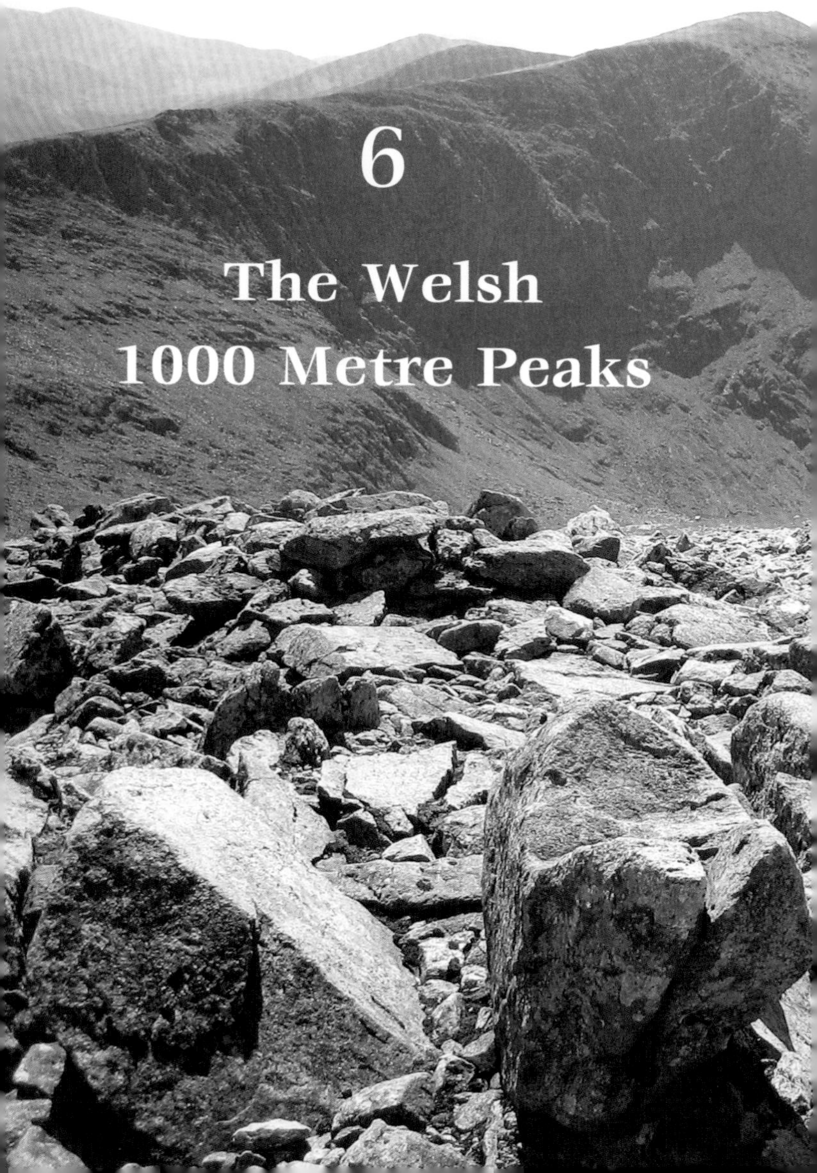

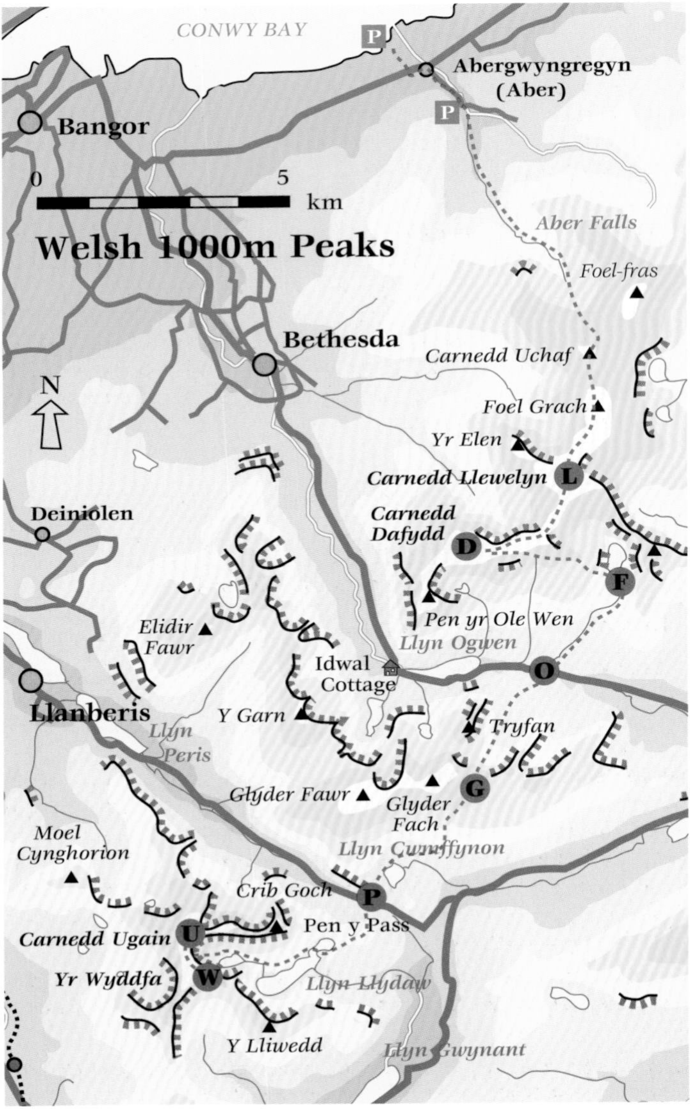
CONWY BAY
P
Abergwyngregyn
(Aber)
P
Bangor
0
5
km
Welsh 1000m Peaks
Aber Falls
Foel-fras
Bethesda
Carnedd Uchaf
N
Foel Grach
Yr Elen
Carnedd Llewelyn
L
Deiniolen
Carnedd
Dafydd
D
F
Pen yr Ole Wen
Elidir
Fawr
Llyn Ogwen
Idwal
Cottage
O
Llanberis
Y Garn
Tryfan
Llyn
Peris
G
Glyder Fawr
Glyder
Fach
Moel
Cynghorion
Llyn Cwmffynon
Crib Goch
P
Pen y Pass
Carnedd Ugain
U
Yr Wyddfa
W
Llyn Llydaw
Y Lliwedd
Llyn Gwynant

After the Second World War the Welch Fusiliers, clad in full battle dress, used the Welsh Three Thousands as a training exercise. As numbers grew they were accused of contributing to the severe erosion on the mountainside and pressure was put on them to find an alternative. They chose the 'One Thousands', a route which visits the four Snowdonian peaks that top 1000m in elevation – Yr Wyddfa and Carnedd Ugain from the Snowdon Group, and Carnedds Llewelyn and Dafydd.

The race route makes an interesting challenge walk, starting as it does from the salty mudflats known as the Lavan Sands and entering the hills by a wooded glen, a magnificent waterfall, and a little-visited back valley. Participants in the annual race will be disqualified if spotted on Crib Goch, but informal walkers can vary the route to take in that and other extra 3000s, or could even continue along the 'Snowdonia to Gower' long-distance route to the Bristol Channel.

The Route	WELSH 1000 METRE PEAKS
Start	Abergwyngregyn (Aber) (SH647731)
Finish	Yr Wyddfa summit SH609543
Distance	35km (22 miles)
Ascent	2700 metres
Time	3 hr 27 min –15 hr

Shorter than the Welsh Three Thousands, this route begins at the car park on the seashore at Aber. It passes southwards through Aber village. A word of warning here (well two actually): be prepared! Since the recent road improvements, the village has been sidelined and affords little opportunity to obtain supplies. There is a good cafe, Hen Felin, but nothing else on the route until the cafe at Pen y Pass.

Follow signs out of **Aber** for Afon Rhaeadr Fawr (river of the big waterfall). After 1.5km (a mile) a small car park beside a

Overleaf: the Black Ladder crags of Carnedd Dafydd, seen from Carnedd Llewelyn. At back left, Yr Wyddfa and Carnnedd Ugain.

The Afon Goch, hidden valley at the head of the Carneddau

stone bridge **Bont Newydd** is reached (£2 a day). Either enter the woodland to the right of the bridge, or cross it and follow a wider path through a gate, towards Aber Falls. The more aesthetic woodland path meets the main path at a wooden kissing gate after a short distance.

After passing under two high power lines, fork left off the wide main path to enter into the darkness of pine woods. After 1km (about 1/2 mile) the easy to follow path emerges at a stile onto the open hillside. A path down right leads to the foot of **Aber Falls**, but the 1000 Metres route slants up across the scree slopes ahead to a short but tricky and damp rock section that weaves its way to the top of the falls. Here the impressive spout plummets 50 metres or so over a rocky precipice and the walker (or runner without the speed or inclination to win races) can look back across the lip to Anglesey and Puffin Island.

The route now enters the wild inner sanctum of the Carneddau via the remote hanging valley of the Afon Goch with its inviting clear rock pools, where sheep tracks trace the east banks of the river (*water source*). Two rocky crests, Llwytmor and Bera Mawr, stand either side of the valley like sentries. The paths that continue for 2km (1 1/2 miles) along the left side of **Afon**

Goch watercourse are obvious to start with, but get confusing after passing some sheepfolds. Large rocks inconveniently placed compel the body to twist and turn, and make conditions underfoot difficult. As the path gains height, keep to the left of a gorge and a mini waterfall, after which the path gets fainter until it virtually disappears among tussocky grasses near the head of the cwm. The final climb out of the valley is unforgiving and the ridge seems to get no nearer each time you look at it for encouragement. Mercifully the path eventually gives up the fight and emerges at the main ridge of the Carneddau between Foel-fras (left) and Carnedd Uchaf (right).

A well-defined path leads over the rocky summit of **Carnedd Uchaf** before tackling the steep grass slopes to **Foel Grach's** boulder-ridden top. Amongst the boulders on its north-east flanks there is a mountain refuge hut, which is useful for those caught out in a storm, but has on too many occasions been used as a place for the ill-mannered to dump their surplus orange peel and Coke cans.

The ridge broadens as it swells to the first 1000 metre peak, **Carnedd Llewelyn** (Control L). Prince Llewelyn's Cairn looks down on that of his little brother Dafydd, while Snowdon and the pointed Elidir Fawr form a backdrop.

The well-used path descends from the summit cairn alongside a wall, south then southwest, to a col separating the hollows of Cwm Llugwy and Cwm Pen-llafar. This area is a favourite haunt of ravens and these menacing looking birds can often be seen scavenging on Llewelyn's crest. The views are channelled down to Bethesda, a village surrounded by piles of discarded slate.

Ysgolion Duon, the Black Ladders, are gigantic climbers' cliffs that seldom see the sun. The route stays close to their tops on its way up the stony slopes to **Carnedd Dafydd** (Control D).

Another peak, Pen yr Ole Wen, lies to the south, but it doesn't reach the required metric figure, so the 1000s turns up its nose and ignores this upstart.

Originally a descent was made directly from Carnedd Dafydd to Ogwen, but due to access problems this has been changed. The new, more circuitous route heads back eastwards to Craig Llugwy. Keep to south of crags on Craig Llugwy and above the west side of the reservoir to reach the unmanned checkpoint Control F (SH694624) at the outlet of the **Ffynnon Llugwy Reservoir** (*water source*). From here the tarmac reservoir approach road declines to the A5, which it reaches 2km east of Llyn Ogwen (Control O, SH687603). (Independent walkers will probably prefer the descent of Pen yr Ole Wen's east ridge, described in Chapter 5.)

Alas, Glyder Fawr is a single metre short of the magical 1000m mark, and the finest range of mountains in Wales are snubbed by this particular challenge. Until of course some mischievous Welshman decides to build a bigger summit cairn.

After crossing the busy A5 road the route continues past **Gwern Gof Isaf** (campsite) up the desolate cwm of **Nant yr Ogof** (*water source*). It climbs out to gain the Glyder ridge at **Llyn Caseg-fraith**, where it joins the old Miners Track. This path traverses the grassy saddle between Glyder Fach and Y Foel Goch (past Control G at SH668578) before descending bouldery slopes towards the inn at Pen y Gwryd. The cascading stream met on the descent is a *water source* with numerous pools to cool the feet. The path should be abandoned at the wall-crossing, and a bee-line made westwards for **Llyn Cwmffynnon**. At the north-west side of the lake, a route that has descended from Glyder Fawr takes you down between the rocks and over a ladder stile to **Pen y Pass Youth Hostel** (Control P), which lies in a barren rocky gorge, the Pass of Llanberis.

From the back right corner of the cafe car park opposite, follow the heavily engineered **Pig Track**, which climbs above the Pass of Llanberis before swinging left to **Bwlch y Moch** at the foot of Crib Goch and overlooking lake-filled Cwm Dyli.

The path now veers right, traversing the scabby lower slopes of Crib Goch and Carnedd Ugain before passing above another lake, this time the blue-green Glaslyn. Here the route climbs friable water-eroded slopes in zigzags (*water source*) to the junction with the Miners Track (Control M SH614548) and then up to the obelisk at **Bwlch Glas**. Here the route is joined by the tourist trail from Llanberis, which includes those cute little trains.

Before heading for Yr Wyddfa, the Welsh 1000s turns right for **Carnedd Ugain** (Control U) and heads north-eastwards to

Glaslyn and Llyn Llydaw, with the Pig Track contouring the slope of Crib Goch above the lakes

its summit. Steps are then retraced to the col before that final climb along the left side of the railway track to **Yr Wyddfa** (Control W).

Sporting History of the 1000m Peaks Race

The 1971 inaugural Welsh 1000 Metres Peak Race had nineteen entrants. The fell runners' class was won by Dennis Weir in 3 hours 47 minutes. In the following year, Joss Naylor won in 3 hours 37 minutes, which was to be his best time. Joss went on to win the race for five consecutive years. Mike Short broke Naylor's record by forty-five seconds in 1978.

In 1979 access problems required the course to be rerouted via Ffynnon Llugwy. Mike Short won the new race in 3 hours 32:59 and dominated the event into the 1980s. Since then the race has been won seven times by Colin Donnelly.

The 1999 race was designated as one of those counting towards the British fell-running championship. This factor, and good weather on the day, made for a very fast race. The winner, Gavin Bland from Borrowdale, brought the record down to 3 hours 27:20. Angela Mudge's time of 4 hours 02:20 reduced the women's record by half an hour. Both records still stand. The 2008 winner was Colin Donnelly, still a champion fully twenty years after his record-breaking run over the Welsh 3000s.

Low cloud in 2000 meant that less than half completed the event within the time limits. In 2007, an unfortunate runner took a bad line at speed down into Cwm Lloer, and fell to his death.

After a slight decline around the turn of the century, when fellrunning fell out of favour generally, the race now is as popular as at any time during its four decades. The race limits are usually filled in early spring soon after entries open.

There are currently six classes in the race:

A Fell Runners (minimum age 18; cut-off time 7hr 30min)
B Mountaineers (with rucksacks, boots and other specified items of equipment; minimum age 17; cut off time 9 hrs, but there is a non-competitive Class **Be** starting 1hr 40 min earlier)
C Mountaineers as B, but starting from Ogwen (minimum age 15)
D As B but for service teams (minimum age 17)
E Fellrunners as A, Ogwen start (minimum age 16)

There are prizes for men, women, veterans (over 40), super-veterans (over 50) and for declared teams.

The race has been officially re-named "The Snowdonia Summits Marathon" but still seems to use the old name mostly. It is now organised jointly by the Gorphwysfa Mountaineering Club and the Army in Wales. It is held on the first Saturday in June. Runners must have completed two previous long fell races and be able to navigate. The organisers provide buses from the Royal Victoria Hotel at Llanberis to the two start points. Shorter courses at lower altitudes have been devised in case of extreme weather conditions.

Entry details are in the information section, Chapter 10.

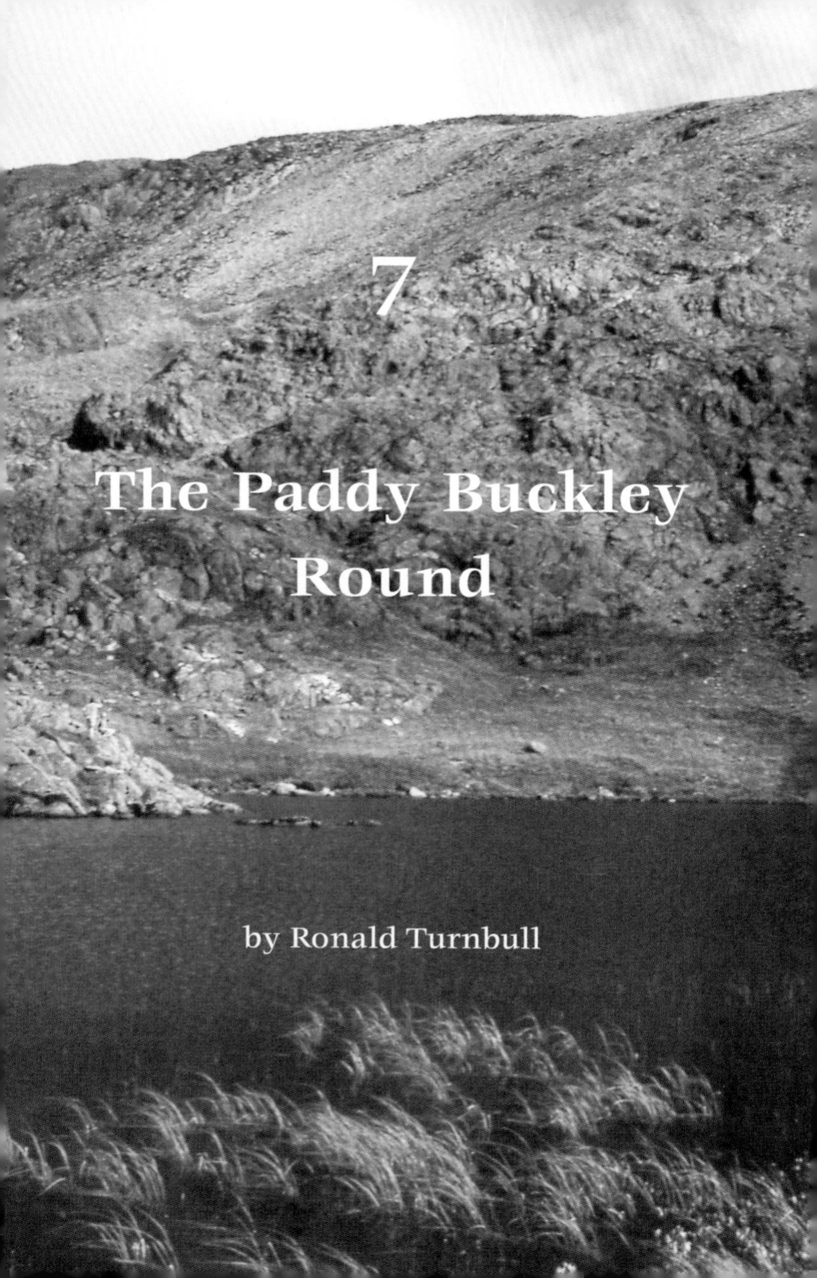

7

The Paddy Buckley Round

by Ronald Turnbull

Descending towards Llyn Bochlwyd. For runners on the Buckley Round, this long descent from Tryfan can be a make-or-break point. Various lines have been tried, including one to the head of Llyn Ogwen.

Overleaf: Llyn y Cwn, the Dog Lake, below Glyder Fawr

Ronald's Round

The ridges of Y Garn and Trum y Ddysgl are nice ... but not at midnight. They're still less nice at midnight in mist. At the top of a long gentle grass ridge, everything just stops. There's a sort of path down on the right, but then things get steeper and steeper, with more and more rocks. The torch shows only a small sphere of grey glare, but there's a feeling of great emptiness all around.

So there I was, crouching to shine my torch onto the boulders to try and tell which ones had been walked on, and ignoring the black hole beyond that could have been six feet of drop, but could equally have been six hundred.

Then at the col the wind blew a brief hole in the cloud, so that I saw unlikely vertical shapes against the sky – which were where I was supposed to go – and distant orange blobs of civilisation – which were where, if I had any sense, I'd already be.

Paddy Buckley's round of forty-seven Snowdonian summits isn't a place for the sensible. 95km (sixty miles) horizontal, and 8700 metres uphill, and involving a certain amount of heather, rock, bog and bracken: all this is just that little bit more than a human being can hope to manage within twenty-four hours. That, of course, is the fun of it.

And fun it was, to start with, as I jogged across the footbridge at Plas y Brenin, with Plas y Brenin's canoeists splashing about in the water below. A quick glance to the right showed a lake with a lot of pretty white waves on, which means, if my nautical forebear is to be believed, that we're looking at Force Five here. Beyond the pretty white waves is a brief glimpse of Snowdon. I can't help noticing that the bottom part of Snowdon is quite a long way away, and the top part of Snowdon's in cloud.

No time for that. I'm in a nicely scented afternoon forest, but they say that smells and memory occupy the same bit of brain and memory's working at high speed here. This is because of the OS Outdoor Leisure map, which has these first three miles printed on the back. The map is inconveniently large. However, the business of refolding it inside out in Force Five will soon reduce it to small manageable-sized pieces scattered all over Snowdonia. So this first three miles is being done on memory and concentration and by looking for footprints in the pine needles.

But soon enough I'm on the open slopes, with the way ahead spread grassy green under the sun, and the only complication is in remembering which of the minor bumps along the fence count towards the forty-seven: to which the answer is 'all of them'. And the ground though low is interesting, and interestingly different from the rest of the Round. Small rocks hold in their hollows sparkling pools or else vicious bits of black bog. A whimsical glacier has sharpened Moel Meirch into a black pencil-point. The path passes by it, but machete-work through the heather bush is rewarded by a ten-second scramble to its rough summit.

But tumbling down the rough grass to the quarries I'm 25 minutes ahead, which is bad: 25 minutes ahead is too fast by far. And mist is wafting across the grey surface of Llyn Conglog,

Moelwyn Bach, seen from the ridge of Cnicht

which is worse – for I've been romantic, or you could call it lazy, and not explored any of this in advance.

John's at the quarries with friendly words and powdered long-distance food. John by car and short walk from Tanygrisiau has reached here a mere ten minutes quicker than me, and this makes me feel briefly to be a real hillrunner. And thus I continue to feel as I scamper the wonderful terraced path across the steeps of Moelwyn Mawr, the path made by miners for the comfort of runners across the rocks and screes, the path with the wild view straight down onto mist.

Alas, it's little use being a hillrunner if you're running the wrong hill. I take an incorrect traverse path from Bwlch Stwlan, and find myself in some particularly inconclusive mist. At the top there's no cairn, but there's only one Moelwyn Bach so I walk the four corners of the plateau and go back down into the inconclusive mist. Various warning signs about deep dangerous holes are ones that warned me on the way up, and I'm pretty sure I'm on the right way back to that Bwlch but better just check the map...

The map shows an isolated contour ring, 300 metres south-east of the summit of Moelwyn Bach. So it's a case of Moelwyn Back we go, to the puddled plateau, and head north-west, and sure enough the ground rises again to somewhere that does have a cairn on it. And right beside that cairn, the quite clear path I should have come up on.

If I knew any blistering Welsh curses I'd be cursing them now. The mist is thick and black, with rain in it, and Moelwyn Mawr's more-or-less OK but there's a long tricky bit across the plateau and a direct route up the south face of Cnicht that no-one in their senses would ever take but only people on the Buckley Round.

I'm just wondering when the south face's going to start getting really steep and nasty when it rolls over like a friendly dog and I'm standing on the ridge path. So what if the ridge is uphill to the right, I know the summit's to the left; and then there's a long gentle runoff, and a rocky craggy place with woods dripping quietly under the bottom edges of the cloud.

After that it's off through some very deep bracken onto a range called the Southern Nantlle, or Eifionydd, or various other things depending on who's doing the calling. That very deep bracken, and a heathery little thing called Y Gyrn (Y Grymace might be more appropriate), and that too fast start, and doing three Moelwyns where the schedule only said two: these were the various reasons why I ended up getting benighted on Y Garn.

Not that that wasn't fun, too. But not the high-intensity 47-in-a-day sort of fun. More disembodied, midnight sort of fun: the Cloud-of-Unknowing sort of fun enjoyed by medieval mountain hermits for whom there's no true virtue in believing the compass reading unless that compass reading's plain impossible.

It was a sort of fun I didn't particularly want a whole lot more of over the rock ridges of Snowdon. So I stopped in the car park, and slept in the parked car until dawn...

Even at dawn, the Snowdon range didn't look attractive. Damp crags had their tops in grey cloud, their feet in brown grass and greenish-brown bog. But having come all the way to Snowdonia, Snowdon is what you have to do. And who knows: the invisible bits up inside the cloud might not be quite so bad as they look.

This turns out to be the case. A grassy edge leads up between two voids of grey air onto Yr Aran. In the col beyond, a silvery pool offers refreshment to the eye and water to the plastic bottle. Clogwyn Du is at its best when the wind blows streamers of mist between the wet little pinnacles. The top of Snowdon is like a seedy theatre at the grey breakfast-time of the morning after, its splendid decoration worn and chipped at the corners, its crowds departed leaving only their empty bottles and crisp wrappers trapped in the cracks of the furniture.

But then on Moel Cynghorion the clouds, which must be connected to a creaky pulley mechanism in the wings, reluctantly rise. The big spotlight in the sky switches on, lakes sparkle like tinsel in windy sunshine, and the wet crags gleam splendidly. It's landscape carved with an axe, this western end of Snowdon. Grass rises towards the sky, turns to give a narrow edge for running along, and then stops abruptly in a sheer drop of a hundred metres or more. The scene displays itself briefly, the curtain drops for half-time; but alas, something jams in the pulley system and the second act never happens.

Llanberis is a town built on slate and of slate, living by slate and possibly even eating slate and watching slate on TV. Rain bounces off the car park with real malevolence as I tuck into a nice tin of creamed rice. Beyond the hedge the surface of the lake lies rain-pocked and grey – slaty grey.

A path winds between high walls into the slate-workings, to look back on Llanberis from directly above. Rare plants grow in the crevices of the workings – downy thistles strangely grey in colour. Elidir Fach is a very ordinary hilltop; however it does have real grass growing out of it.

Elidir Fawr is not ordinary, but a fine rocky ridge, even if it does look down on that strangely circular little reservoir Marchlyn Mawr with its tarred access road. And man's puny attempts at mountain demolition are finally forgotten along the Glyders. For here the landscape has been demolished by glaciers, glaciers which have gouged great hollows into the northern slopes and left their rubble all along the Round's second Foel Goch, its second Y Garn.

Glyder Fawr is another of those places you don't really get the point of until you visit it in mist. All those little rocky bits sticking out of the boulder field: what are they actually for, and why so many? They stand there as a lesson in shape awareness.

Glyder Fach's summit rockpile, and Castell y Gwynt, seen from Bwlch y Ddwy Glyder (photo: James Clayton)

You never appreciate a sculpture until you prowl round it in mist, wondering if it's a totally new one or the one you saw before from the other side. The one that actually is the summit is the second most north-westerly one, and it has a summit cairn, honest it does, on a little platform half way down and round the back where you only see it once you've walked past it convinced that one of the others must be higher.

Glyder Fach is more straightforward. Castell y Gwynt's a jammed logpile, except the logs are stones, and the Cantilever's a seesaw that if it ever swung would shake your bones right out of their sockets. Glyder Fach's an adventure playground for grownups, and when you fall among these boulders there's no mother coming with iodine for your grazed knees. What's coming for you is the Ogwen Valley Rescue Team with their inflatable splint and their stretcher. They won't say 'it'll only hurt for a moment', they won't say anything at all, but they'll silently note down in their notebook that you carried no whistle or survival bag, and that the shoes you were wearing were running shoes.

A nearby spiky place is the top of Bristly Ridge. Really I should be going down Bristly Ridge; but though the 24 hours is an abandoned hope, there's a more pressing cut-off time ahead. Just six more hours to the dusk of the second night, and five Carnedds still to do, and before the five Carnedds, Tryfan.

Pen yr Helgi Du from the slopes of Pen Llithrig y Wrach

Tryfan is wet, and also windy. The few people on Tryfan are clinging to its sides like barnacles on a sea washed rock. It's an awkward clamber up Tryfan's streaming boulders in clothes stiffened by the weight of absorbed rainwater, and an even more awkward clamber down. Hillrunners – real hillrunners – have descended Tryfan to the lakeside in seven minutes dead, or, even harder to credit, in seven minutes still alive. I take roughly seven times those seven minutes, and over the jagged lid of another tin of rice, look to something more straightforward: a simple pull up Pen yr Ole Wen.

Forward – and upward. Except that the top half of it's hidden by the roof of the car. This final climb onto the Carneddau is two thousand two hundred feet in under a mile (650 metres up in just twice that distance across the map). It says: "What are you, a man or a mouse? Me, I'm a mountain."

Higher up, it's scree, and optimistic pressing upward through little gullies between the crags. And now there's real wind, and quite a lot of it: so that I stop thinking 'a tin of rice inside and five hours till dark, I'll finish it anyway,' start thinking about the clifftop of the Ysgolion Duon and whether to get blown over it. Certainly the Ysgolion Duon lie north of my route while the wind is from the south. And the wind is of the blow-me-down variety, bringing me to a bent halt on the stony ridges of David's Carnedd.

Now I haven't been able to track down a Patron Saint of hillrunners, but undoubtedly there must be one. Whoever it was had a rare bit of fun that afternoon on receiving my unspoken prayer: 'Just some ordinary rain and mist, I'm used to that stuff, but how about a break from this wind tunnel bit?'

The wind dropped, became a mere nothing, allowed me even to crouch behind the cairn of Llewelyn's Carnedd and turn the beastly map inside out. And the mist descended: a good thick 'now how's your map-and-compass work' sort of mist. And it rained. It rained a real '... with your map turned to papier mache' sort of rain. It ran in streams down the rocks and up the sleeves of my waterproofs, and turned path to instant mud.

Maybe some lesser saint was having a good laugh, but I was having fun too. Compass work I can do; hillrunning clothes are meant to be soaking wet. And up to Pen yr Helgi Du is one last bit of lovely ridge, rocks and a winding path and two big drops.

And so to the final hill, and down long heather, and out of the simplicity of a compass bearing and a few yards of wet hill and back to the real world. The real world turned out to be a wide empty place, very flat, with a bit of hillside in the distance and no sign of any of the features that look so significant on the OL map such as the Llugwy valley, or the A5(T). Instead there was a whole lot of waist-high heather.

After a brief but intimate encounter with the heather I found the ancient bridleway, and even the A5(T), and trotted down the road to Plas y Brenin.

At the Plas they were skiing: skiing in the dark on a soaking wet dry ski slope. Some people's idea of sport, strange isn't it?

John and his car, having been there faithfully through two days and a night, now weren't. I was soaking wet, with three Mars bars, £20 and a phone card. The £20 would buy Bed & Breakfast and the Bed at least would be dry, though what to wear to eat the Breakfast in was going to be a problem. But the first thing was to eat the Mars bars. By which time John and his car were there after all. I climbed into some dry clothes and we started driving back towards Scotland.

Backpack of the Buckley Round

For fellrunners, the big day out in Wales is the Buckley Round. For walkers, the round is the big day out – then the other big day out – and then the third, and the fourth big days out.

Taken as a backpack trip over four or five days, the Buckley Round is big horizontally – 111km with 9500m of ascent (70 miles and 32,000ft). It's big vertically – Snowdon's just an incident in the early hours of Day 2. Most of all, it's a big experience of intensive Snowdonia. All of the high and sharp ridges are walked with the exception of Crib Goch – but you've probably already done Crib Goch. Eight mountain lakes are visited, and two of the nicest of them are slept beside. Sudden edges are looked over, waterfalls are strolled beside, and beneath the shining slates of Llanberis chips are eaten.

Be reassured: you won't have completely used up Snowdonia when you're through. The northern Carneddau are not visited, there's still Y Lliwedd on the Snowdon Horseshoe, and, yes, one or two tops at the western end of Nantlle.

The route falls into five stages, between road crossings (all of which are on the Sherpa bus routes).

Paddy Buckley Round

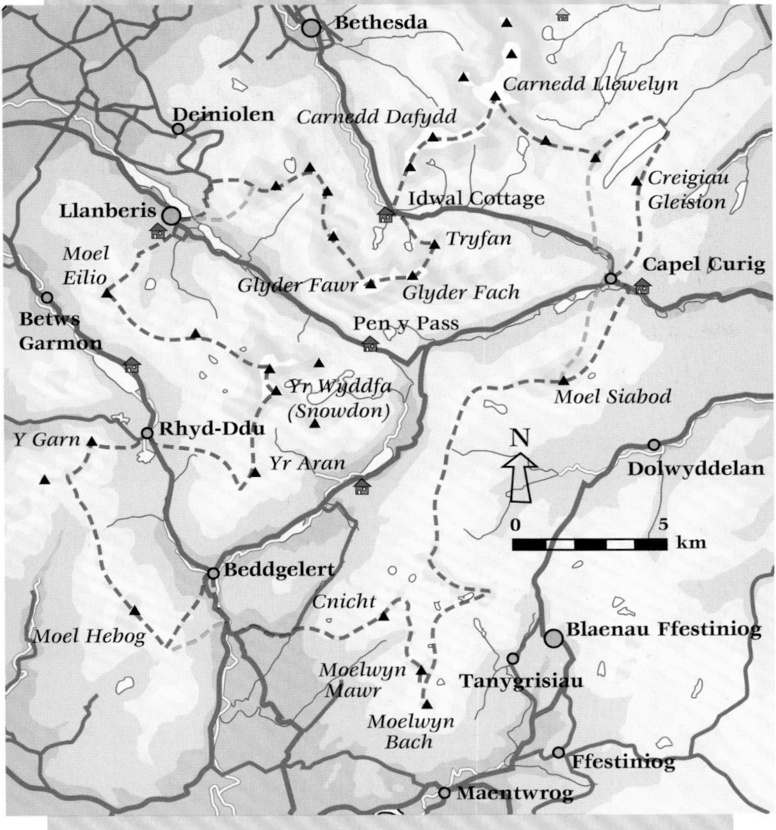

	Paddy Buckley Round	
1.	Rhyd-ddu to Llanberis	20km 1900m (13 miles 6300ft)
	all facilities	
2.	Llanberis to Idwal Cottage	16.5km 1800m (10 miles 6000ft)
	Youth Hostel, snack bar	
3.	Idwal Cottage to Capel Curig YH	20km 1700m (12 1/2 miles 5700ft)
	Youth Hostel, bunkhouse, camp site, pubs, shop	
4.	Capel Curig to Beddgelert	38.5km 2450m (24 miles 8200ft)
	pubs, shop	
5.	Beddgelert to Rhyd-ddu	15.5km 1600m (9 1/2 miles 5300ft)
	pub, bunkhouse, camp site, Youth Hostel (2km)	

Runners take the shortest line, irrespective of nastiness, but the route here is sometimes gentler and slightly longer; also it extends the Carnedd section over six bonus peaks. That's why there's an extra 12km (8 miles).

Tough and ambitious backpackers will aim to pass through the staging points at lunchtime so as to find a bar meal and an open shop, then camp high on the summits or at a sheltered lake. For them, a start at Rhyd-ddu gives, in effect, an extra supply point, as they arrive with food already on their backs. A circuit of this steep and rugged route while carrying overnight gear will only be enjoyed by the strong and fit. Survive this still smiling and the GR20 across Corsica, or the John Muir Trail in California, will seem like comfortable outings (apart from their lack of Wales' cooling rainfall).

For those arriving by car, Llanberis is probably the easiest point to find street parking rather than the ubiquitous pay-and-display. It would be churlish to occupy Capel Curig's free, but small, car park over four full days.

The five staging points almost allow a five-day tour without a tent. The problem here is the excessive day between Capel Curig and Beddgelert. One solution is to divert from Allt-fawr to Blaenau Ffestiniog, where there are one or two B&Bs, a hotel and shops. Another ploy is to start from Capel Curig, break this section with a high camp, and then cache the heavy gear in the woods of Aberglaslyn for later collection. Alternatively, start at Aberglaslyn (saving the diversion to Beddgelert and about 3km!) having previously dumped the tent at Capel Curig.

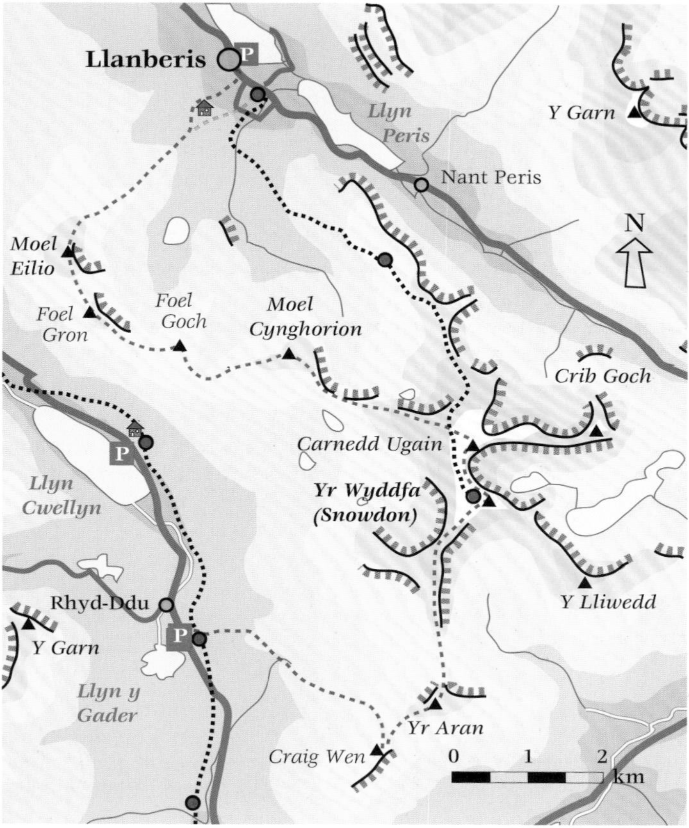

Stage 1 SNOWDON

Rydd-ddu to Llanberis

13 miles (20km) height gain: 6100ft (1800m)

Rhyd-ddu can be reached from Caernarfon by Sherpa bus or, more romantically, by the Welsh Mountain Railway. The Cwellyn Arms has a bunkhouse and campsite, and the Snowdon Ranger YH is 2km to the north. There is no shop. The main car park, at the station, is pay-and-display.

My Welsh phrase books suggest 'Rhyd-ddu' should sound like Rid-Thee or Rid-Thy. My bus driver couldn't understand my Rid-Thee, even though it was the next stop up from Beddgelert – and said it roughly as Rid-Thoo or Rid-They. 'Rid-Thoo', though certainly incorrect, should be understood by both Welsh and English speakers.

From the left end of the car park take a tarred track for 100 metres north. Cross the railway, and in 200 metres fork right (signed 'Snowdon') past a barrier. 1.5km (a mile) from the car park keep straight ahead when the popular Rhyd-ddu Path up Snowdon turns left.

Once over the stream at 350m altitude, continue for 200 metres to a gate, then strike south-east across open moor. Cross two streams, the second with a wall alongside (or, further up the slope, a fence). Slant uphill, still southeast. A fence leads up into the col north of Craig Wen, where it rather surprisingly just ends.

Turn right on a small path alongside occasional iron fence posts, to reach **Craig Wen**'s 608m summit a few minutes away south-west. A small cairn of quartz lumps marks the top. There are comfy hollows here to sleep in, though not if the wind's really strong.

Return along the small path, which leads up the fine grass ridge onto **Yr Aran**. The descent of Yr Aran is steep, and could give trouble even if you've not got benighted. A path, along with the ancient fence remains, descends the north-east ridge, to meet a broken-down stone wall. Here the path contours left (west) for 250 metres, just above the wall, to reach the northern spur of the mountain. Path and wall turn downhill, to the col **Bwlch Cwm Llan** with its small pool. The wall leads on over a knoll to a second col, marked with a cairn, where a right of way crosses the ridge.

A couple of minutes down to the left, two high-perched tarns look out through the gap of the Nantlle valley to the sea. In that sea you should see reflected the sunset of a long and golden day. But in wilder weather, the tarn half a mile north will be more sheltered. In worse weather than that, you can descend eastward on a path that starts steep and loose, but becomes a grass tramway along the Cwm Llan. Nantgwynant has B&Bs, camp sites, an independent hostel and a Youth Hostel.

From the cairned col, follow the broken wall on up the fine sharpness of Snowdon's South Ridge. Soon, a well-built path joins from the right, out of Cwm Llan. The cairn of the minor summit Allt Maenderyn is notable as the point where somewhat slippery slate underfoot gives way to more grippy volcanic rocks. After a ladder stile, the path climbs more steeply, with a scrambling moment even, to the ridge levelling at 931m. Here the summit Cribau Tregalan is uncairned, just above the path, which here runs along to left of the crest.

In another 200 metres, the broad Rhyd-ddu path slides in from below. The combined path now runs cosily, just to the right of the crest, high above Cwm Tregalan. After passing the upstanding rock at the top of the Watkin Path, the wide path wanders left of the scrambly crest, then back to the right. It edges up to right of Hafod Eryri, Snowdon's new hotel and station, to **Y Wyddfa** summit.

Supposing you camped in the Bwlch Cwm Llan, sunrise now blazes behind the jagged crest of Y Lliwedd, and at 8:00 am there's no need to queue for the privilege of sitting on Snowdon's summit trig. In two or three hours this'll become a busy and cheerful place, with ice creams and a dear little toy train. But when dawn shadows fill the valleys of mankind, Snowdon summit returns to a time when eagles really did nest in Eryri.

Moel Cynghorion and Foel Goch from the Llanberis Path

Scamper down the large built path to the obelisk at the top of the Pig Track (998m spot height), and up a well-trodden path to **Carnedd Ugain** – the quickest trig-to-trig in Wales. Drop west to cross stone-fields and grass, the wide Llanberis Path, and then the railway, to the wide Snowdon Ranger Path just below. Descend its zig-zags, or the crest on the right, to **Llyn Ffynnon-y-gwas**.

Above the path is a col with a ladder stile. In very thick mist you might fail to see the ladder stile or, indeed, the lake. When the path levels to cross a stream culvert (SH586557) you have overshot by 300 metres; but the stream is a valuable water point anyway.

A small path wanders up the fence line over **Moel Cynghorion**, whose summit has a ladder stile and a vestige of cairn. Crags are all around but you're on the gentlest of grass, with the fence alongside to guide you. It's a place to linger on a warm forenoon and watch the sparkling of the waters in Cwm Clogwyn. Once down Moel Cynghorion, cross a wall on the right by ladder stile for the fence northwest up **Foel Goch**. Its summit cairn is tiny, just beyond a fence junction.

Return to a ladder stile to follow a new fence west. When that turns away, continue west then northwest through a col.

The map has the summit of Foel Gron at 593m, but the point 400 metres northwest, where the ridgeline fence restarts, is more convincingly a separate top. Its uncairned grass knob, teetering on the brink of a terrific crag, gives a brief moment of non-tranquillity in this grassy afternoon. Follow more fences northwest to the big shelter on **Moel Eilio**.

Perched on the end of the range, this is a softer sort of mountain. Look back along the ridge to Snowdon, marvelling at how far you've come, and ignore for now the dark Glyders laid out for your consideration along the far side of Nant Peris.

Follow the fence northward for 400 metres, to the fence junction at 650m. Bear right alongside the side-fence. The fence, and a small path (one either side) lead down the north-east ridge, with handsome ladder-stiles at every cross-fence. At 250m a stile leads onto a horizontal cross-track. Turn right for 200 metres. A gate on the left opens onto the tarred lane above the Youth Hostel.

You could follow the lane down to the Youth Hostel (and small camp site) and Llanberis village centre. But for a short cut that's easy on the feet and also on the eye, descend the lane for only a few steps past the first house. Below its gate, a red-top post marks a path descending to the right of the lane beside a wall. After a kissing gate, bear slightly right down to a second gate beside a stream. Continue beside the stream towards a kissing gate on the left near houses, but don't go through that gate. Instead turn downhill past another waymarker, to right of a wall, to join a tarred track that leads downhill beside the railway. A fine waterfall is beyond; a first level crossing on the right could take you to the fall's top, while a second one gives a partial view of the fall itself between trees.

Continue down the tarred lane to the top of Llanberis. Bear right towards the railway's viaduct, but then turn left through a play area to a tarred path at its bottom left corner. Bear half-right, downhill among houses, with a river nearby on the right, to emerge on the A4086 just west of the bottom station of the Snowdon Mountain Railway.

The village centre is on the left; the following section starts along the road opposite, signed to the slate museum.

Llanberis has a youth hostel and camp site, a bunkhouse at the Heights Hotel, and a late-opening Spar shop.

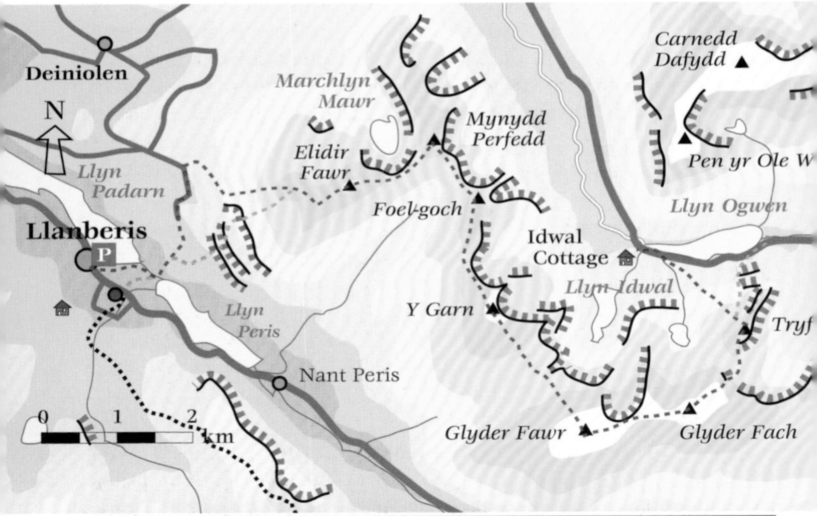

Stage 2 GLYDERAU

Llanberis to Idwal Cottage (Llyn Ogwen)

10 miles (16.5km) height gain: 6000ft (1800m)

From the A4086 just west of the Snowdon Mountain Railway's bottom station, a road signed to the slate museum leads to the bridge between Llyn Padarn and Llyn Peris (SH587600).

From Llanberis village, there's a pleasanter way. At the foot of the Youth Hostel's downhill lane, turn left for 120 metres, across Afon Goch (river), then turn right in a lane just past the Heights Hotel and opposite the Spar shop. Cross A4068 onto a lakeside footpath, that runs behind a car park (SH580602, west of the Electric Mountain car park). The path leads to a footbridge (SH586602) alongside a railway. Cross, and turn right for 200 metres to the end of the road bridge.

Opposite the road bridge, a footpath zigzags up through trees and slate-workings, marked with blue/yellow topped posts. There's a fine view back over the slate piles to the rooftops of Llanberis and the grey waters of its lake. The path crosses a metal footbridge over a trackbed – that trackbed is the direct, ugly route through the quarries used by Buckley Round runners in a hurry. But keep on up the path, bearing left, uphill, past a turnoff for the Anglesey Barracks. At a noticeboard of various Padarn perils, the blue-yellow posts bear up left but bear right onto a track to the first houses of **Dinorwig**.

Keep ahead through the village on a tarred lane. This passes a car park where a footpath to the right would lead back into the slate workings. But stay on the road for another 500 metres as it contours around northwest. At a BT phone box (possibly soon to be removed) and just before a stone shed, a footpath sign points up into a little walled path. Follow this uphill to a rough track. Turn right on this for 20 metres to a kissing gate, where the path continues uphill to a tarred lane.

Turn right, following the lane to its end at a turning area below slate piles. Head up the field beyond, then up the foot of the slate piles, to a water board road with crash barrier. Cross this and continue uphill to the two cairns at the summit of **Elidir Fach**.

Cross the wide col east to join a fence, which runs up towards the minor southwest summit of Elidir Fawr but stops short just before reaching it. Work round left into a small col, and follow the bouldery crest to the summit of **Elidir Fawr**.

The Glyders now lie before you. To start with, they'll be an ordinary bit of nice ridge, with long slopes rising to a crest. It's after Llyn y Cwn that things are going to get rocky.

The path slants east down Elidir's Fawr's southern flank. Where it rejoins the ridgeline there's a burst of quartz veins, boiled out of the rocks by the heat of the microgranite intrusion of Mynydd Perfedd ahead. The ridge narrows across the col high above Marchlyn Mawr. There's a rocky scramble along the top if you want it, but a path down on the right as well. That path on the right doesn't just avoid the scrambly bits, it avoids Mynydd Perfedd as well. So pass below the col but then leave the path as soon as it has grass above it, slanting up to a fence that leads up northeast. The summit of **Mynydd Perfedd** is beyond the fence: the microgranite's main feature is not having slaty cleavage but being blocky.

Recross the fence to descend by a path to its right, to rejoin the main path in the next col. But the path is after the three-thousanders, and now it wants to avoid Foel-goch as well. So leave it immediately after the col to strike left up the scree above on faint zig-zags.

Foel-goch is more glacier-hacked landscape. Here the northern half of the mountain's been taken away and instead you get a 750m hole with a sparkling river in the bottom. It's an effect seen already on Snowdon's Foel Gron, and will be seen again on Mynydd Drws-y-coed; but if you're tired of the sudden missing mountainside you're tired of life. In which case, the north edge of Foel-goch is an ideally convenient spot to fling yourself off despairingly. The cairn has been removed from the crag brink to a lower, safer spot within the fence.

Walk the gentle plateau southwards, following the decayed fence, to rejoin that three-thousanding path that doesn't know what it's missed. Let it take you up Y Garn. Just beyond the summit there's an area of quartz nodules like projecting knuckles, and the path for the next few metres is a rolling surface of rounded quartz. It is rather eroded down the back of Y Garn and over a ladder stile to the **Llyn y Cwn** or 'Dog Lake'.

As the path passes to left of the lake, the built path left (northwards) is the last easy escape to Ogwen in case night's threatening to fall before you really wanted it to. For from here, Glyder stops being like anywhere you've been so far. From here, it's stones and rocks all the way. The stones are big ones, and arranged into peculiar shapes. And the rocks congeal into crags, to make this fractured plateau an awkward place to get away from.

Stones and rocks make for a long tough pull up the slope east of Llyn y Cwn. The rough scree-path slants up left-to-right through crags, then zigzags up scree. Once the slope eases, it crosses stones, marked with sprawling cairns. The line is southeast across the stonefield, then as the path comes onto rocks and passes a 7-finger tor (50 metres right of path) it turns slightly north of east.

Boulders mostly lie flat on the ground, but on the Glyder plateau they've applied some sort of high-altitude hair gel and are determined to stick up just as high as they possibly can. Glyder Fawr has half a dozen of these little rocky surprises. The true summit is the second one to left of the path – perhaps. It appears divided in two from this approach.

Splintered boulders, cairns and a path head just north of east across the plateau, to run alongside the northern drops. In the same direction the path crosses gravelly ground, then drops slightly below the crest to run just below, south, of the col **Bwlch y Ddwy Glyder**.

Another few steps slanting downhill, and then round to the right on the southern slope, then up, is the way to avoid the outcrop of **Castell y Gwynt**. Watch out for worn tops on the boulders to guide you, and short sections of gravelly path. Once on the plateau, with the Castell's jammed boulderpile on your left, turn back east. **Glyder Fach**'s summit lumps are extremely classy ones but there are only three of them, so you shouldn't get too confused. Well, not unless you're looking for the non-existent trig point the old Outdoor Leisure Map playfully placed

Looking back from Tryfan towards Bristly Ridge, and (to its left) the screes of the usual descent route from Glyder Fach

on the true summit. That summit is a heap of boulders with holes in. If you brought a trained marmot, you could retrieve many valuable compasses and woolly hats from the interior of the pile.

Continue just north of east (but don't take bearings while standing on the rockpile itself, in case of dropping the compass!) Pass left of the famous Cantilever and continue for 300 metres to pass the spiky outcrop that's the top of Bristly Ridge. From a large cairn, go down eroded scree immediately beyond. (Or else scramble down Bristly Ridge, of course.)

After zigzagging down northeast, the paths combine to slant down leftwards below the rocks of Bristly Ridge. Level with its base, follow a wall ahead down into Bwlch Tryfan.

Follow the path through the col, crossing one of its ladder stiles on the way. Take the first rocks direct, or, more easily, slant up the left flank by paths and boulder-scrambles.

A section of stone wall crosses the small col (SH663592) behind Tryfan's Far South Summit. (The ladder stile over this wall leads to the top of the Heather Terrace path). From this col, the easiest way is again by paths and boulders about 200 metres round on the left flank.

Once on the crest, a sudden emptiness ahead marks the top of the eastern cliffs. After the slight drop between South Summit and the main one, head up to the two upright rocks that are **Tryfan**'s summit.

Is the proper climax to a backpack such as this, to leap from Adam to Eve while wearing the full long-distance rucksack? I didn't fancy it myself.

Keep ahead, dropping into a col (ahead of it being the slight rise to North Top). From just below and left of the true col, an open gully of boulders heads down left, west. It's steep but well-trodden with occasional boulder scrambles – probably the most straightforward, if not the pleasantest, Tryfan route up or down.

The gully opens to a boulder slope. At its foot, a built path descends steepish grass. From the foot of this, as the slope eases at about the 400m contour, fork left on a faint grass path. This heads down a gentle spurline to the foot of the stream below

Llyn Bochlwyd. Cross a ladder stile (SH653603) onto the A5, and follow pavement to Ogwen Cottage.

Here are Idwal Cottage Youth Hostel, a pay-and-display car park, and a snack bar.

Stage 3 CARNEDDAU

Idwal Cottage to Capel Curig

12½ miles (20km) height gain: 5700ft (1700m)

The Carneddau are high and stony. The drops over the Ysgolion Duon are quite exciting, until you get to the really exciting ridge to Pen yr Helgi Du: here the drops are on both sides at once. Take afternoon tea at Capel Curig before climbing the dramatic dolerite of Moel Siabod's eastern cwm.

Six hundred and fifty metres up Pen yr Ole Wen is just a matter of getting on with it. Cross the A5 bridge to the Alf Embleton memorial stile, for a signed path up the south ridge. The way starts up a rock crack slightly left. For the first 100m or so of height gain the path is very steep, and has been reconstructed by the path-reconstruction people. Above that it's loose scree and boulders, while remaining very steep. Towards the top it traverses right, into the bottom of a well-worn rocky groove. The rocky groove is – need it be said? – very steep. It's a cruel place, where much effort is rewarded only with splendid views of the A5 trunk road.

It's worth it when you get up. Broad stony cragtops lead over the next five miles (8km), with not very much uphill at all, and lots of cragtops to peer over. From the shelter cairn at the top of the steep ascent, enjoy the flatness as you stroll 300 metres north-east to **Pen yr Ole Wen's** actual summit.

Now a broad stony ridge leads round the head of an eastern cwm to a huge bronze-age cairn (which isn't the top of **Carnedd Dafydd**), and to a slightly smaller contemporary cairn (which is). Continue eastward along the top of the Ysgolion Duon – in wild weather the path slightly down right of the clifftop edge may be preferred. But return to the crest at the point where it dips and turns south-east. Here, just over the northern edge, a

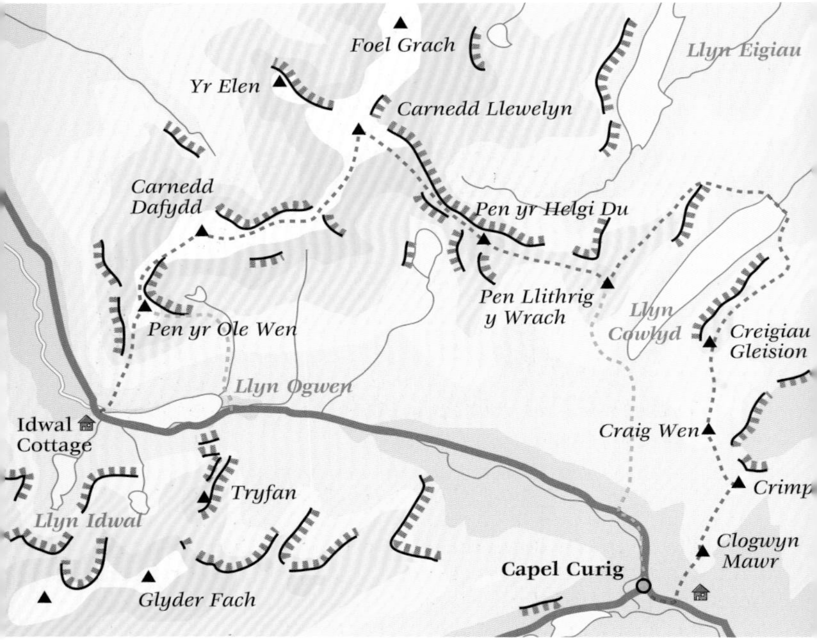

sharpish rocky ridge springs out. This leads northeast, onto the broad shoulder of Carnedd Llewelyn.

Llewelyn itself is a wide flat-topped heap of stones. Long green valleys slide out quietly in various directions, like serpents leaving the ruins of an ancient temple.

A big shelter cairn marks the summit of **Carnedd Llewelyn**. Head southeast for 30 metres to a middle-sized cairn marking the top of the pathed descent ridge. It runs down quite steeply, turning east then back southeast. The ridge levels and becomes grassy. Don't relax too much: the crags of Craig yr Ysfa drop fearsomely on the left, and sharpness and rockiness increase considerably on the approach to the col, with some simple down-scrambling to be done into **Bwlch Eryl Farchog**.

From the low point of the col, an escape-route stony path zigzags down right, towards Llugwy reservoir. Through the col

On the west ridge of Pen yr Helgi Du

itself and onward towards Pen yr Helgi Du, the ridge is fine and narrow. Do not be misled by traverse paths on the right, which head off unhelpfully down the south ridge; take the crest direct. After wrestling with the rocks you emerge onto the peaceful green place that's **Helgi Du's** summit. Down southeast, gentle ridge and a small path lead down to a low pass. It's the **Bwlch y Tri Marchog**: an ancient through route from the heart of Snowdonia to the sea.

Now the credit balance you built up on Pen yr Ole Wen is used up. After the ladder stile, it's a stiff 180m climb up a small path to the summit of **Pen Llithrig y Wrach**.

From here the Buckley Round route runs off southwestwards to Capel Curig *(see route description in Section 9)*. But the backpack route heads northwest for some rough, remote, buzzard country above Llyn Cowlyd. After all, your only excuse for taking five days rather than 24 hours is that you're taking in the six extra summits to east of the reservoir.

From here, if it's clear, you can see that across Llyn Cowlwyd is a new kind of country. Softer slate rocks are stiffened with dolerite sills – intrusions of volcanic basalt forming great slabs of crag. The sills, originally flat and level, have been tilted by later earth movements.

Wiggle the shoulders under the painful backpack, and head down northeast on a small, peaty path. At the wide col at 560m, the path turns north, but here head down rough ground towards the reservoir. On this descent, I was assaulted suddenly and several times by a swooping buzzard. Most alarming was when it zoomed in from behind: I was seriously concerned that my wooly hat might end up tangled in its talons.

If the ground steepens below, head round to the left a little, to reach rough grassland with a fence running downhill. Pass a ladder stile where a bridleway crosses the fence, but keep downhill to the track above the shoreline. Turn left to a very rough hut (open to humans and sheep, which leaves the nastier mess?) and a locked one, at the dam end of **Llyn Cowlyd**.

A track crosses below the dam, with a path up to the dam's east corner. Follow the shoreline for 400 metres, until a fence heads uphill. Keep 20 - 50 metres to left of this fence, finding traces of path, up the first steep bracken, heather, and stones. As the slope eases, above crags on the right, the buzzard stops dive-bombing and a clearer path is found, running still to left of the fence to a fence bend at the ridgeline (SH736624). Here a clearer path arrives along the fence from down ahead.

Pass through a fence gap on the combined path, which is peaty as you follow it west to the 634m Northeast Top of Creigiau Gleision, which is formed from two dolerite sills dipping northeast. The small path circles just below the summit, then drops to a col, with a large quartz outcrop just below. It leads on along a knolly ridge, southwest, to the 678m true top of **Creigiau Gleision**. Another big dolerite sill makes up this summit. Accordingly the rock is compact, smooth, and rather holdless, giving a more austere sort of scramble than the tuffs and lavas of the Glyders or Snowdon.

The peaty path runs down south to **Craiglwyn**. Then it heads down southwest, avoiding a rocky knoll up on its left, to cross a wide soggy col and skirt the west flank of Craig Wen, keeping below the rocky summit knolls. The true summit of **Craig Wen** (548m) is at the centre of the plateau. It's reached slightly awkwardly up low dolerite walls, or else spiral around. 200 metres south, the cairned south summit has great views.

Head down west to regain the flanking path, and follow it down southeast, joining a broken wall into the col before Crimpiau. The path heads steeply uphill, with crags above and to left. A pleasant bare rock knoll forms **Crimpiau** summit.

Now a peaty path ahead descends east, and should eventually join a wide smooth path down Nant y Geuallt. For a more direct (but rougher) route, head down southwest, over bilberry and outcrops, following the ill-defined ridgeline towards **Llyn y Coryn**. A soggy path passes 100 metres left of the tarn, then joins a fence running down southwest. Where this bends down left, keep ahead down the broad, wet, rough, ill defined ridgeline to its final hummock, **Clogwyn-mawr**. It's a splendid viewpoint overlooking Capel Curig.

Descend west, on small path, to a ladder stile. Now a steep path heads directly downhill, over another ladder stile, to meet a broad path connecting various parts of Capel Curig. Go across it and continue straight downhill to a ladder stile at the slope foot. Ignore yet another ladder stile on the right into a camp site, but keep ahead through the camp site's parking yard to reach the A5 200 metres west of **Capel Curig Youth Hostel**.

Capel Curig has a bunkhouse at the camp site, and another in the village, where there are also three pubs. The A4086 crossroads, 800 metres to the west, has the Pinnacle Café and stores, with more supplies at the garage at the east end of the village. Or there's a 600m climb up Siabod dead ahead.

Stage 4 MOELWYNS & CNICHT

Capel Curig to Beddgelert

24 miles (38.5km)   height gain: 8200ft (2450m)

Snowdonia north of the A498 is big simple shapes carved by glaciers. This southern country is different – different from the North and not even the same as itself, so that at one minute you're on the ridge and the next it's 50m away. The rock is close to the surface and in its hollows it holds evil little bogs or perfect pools.

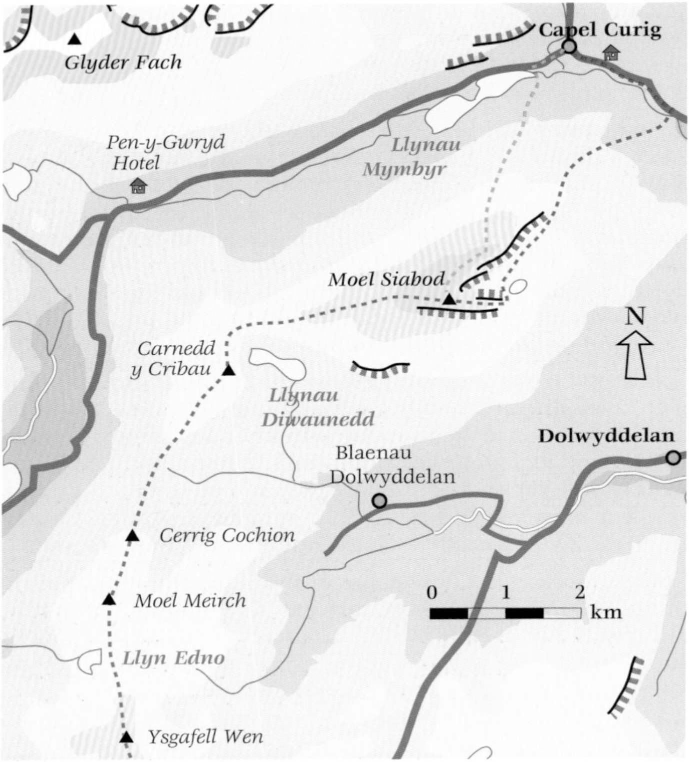

Along this eastern range, the older, softer rocks form the moorland slopes. The tops are formed from the younger and tougher volcanic rocks. But each of the tough tops is a bit different: pale rhyolite lavaflows on Cerrig Cochion, black underwater basalt on the side of Carnedd y Cribau, dolerite on Moel Siabod.

On Moel Siabod's east ridge

There are four plausible ways up Moel Siabod; the grassy northern flank, and then three different ways to tackle the rocky eastern approach.

Summit of Moel Siabod

1. **The northern route from Plas y Brenin** is quickest. It is, however, an insult to Moel Siabod, as it totally ignores its authentic eastern side. Apart from Buckley runners in a hurry, it's the route for those who don't actually like mountains much.

Just west of the Activity Centre at Plas-y-Brenin, a footpath sign points down left. (Verge parking here in 2008 will soon be blocked off.) Look to your right as you cross the footbridge over the Llynnau Mymbyr – and what you get depends on the weather. It could be a striking view into the heart of Snowdon's eastern cwm; or it could be grey cloud, whitecaps and a faceful of spray.

A nice sheltered path leads up through the woods. At the horizontal track turn left for a few steps, then up to the left of a stream, to emerge from the trees at a stile.

A slaty path leads over a ladder stile and up the hill flank. After passing below a rocky (dolerite) crest it joins the main ridge and disappears for the last 400 metres to Moel Siabod's dolerite-perched trig.

---

2. **East ridge (Daear Ddu)** Siabod's east ridge is a dramatic approach by quarry pool and crag base, followed by a fine easy scramble. (Options 3 and 4 are ways of avoiding the scramble.)

Follow pavement east out of Capel Curig to Cobden's Hotel. Opposite it, cross a handsome footbridge over the rocks and small falls of **Afon Llugwy**. Scramble down left to join a rough path alongside the river (or keep ahead to a signpost a few steps ahead and double back). The path emerges from woods into open fields, bears slightly away from the river to a small footbridge, and joins a driveway where you turn left towards a road bridge over the river, the **Pont Cyfyng**.

Turn right, away from the bridge, past houses, and take the first lane on the right. This winds uphill, marked 'no bikes, no cars' as its indication that walkers are entirely entitled here. The unwelcoming messages are repeated in paint on the tarmac.

As the lane emerges from woodland into bracken, it takes a sharp right, and here a diversionary footpath keeps ahead, well built through the bracken. It bends right to pass above a farm and rejoin what is now a rough track uphill.

The ladder stile sign offering to shoot your dog has now been removed, or else rotted off and awaits replacement. The farm apparently has lambing 12 months in the year, a sloppy practice.

The track runs up towards Moel Siabod. After passing a quarry (out of sight on the left) the main track bends slightly left to a gate and ladder stile. A wide old path continues below the steep-sided northeast ridge and to the right of a reservoir tarn and then a slate spoilheap. The path passes up to the left of a flooded quarry and becomes eroded as it rises to a slight col where, suddenly, **Llyn y Foel** appears in its hollow ahead.

The direct path crosses swampy ground next to the lake, to reach the foot of Siabod's gently-angled but rocky east ridge. From the slight col before the lake an alternate, smaller, path circles to the right, contouring above the swamp (Option 4 turns off here), to join the ridge slightly above its foot.

The ridge crest offers some blocky scrambling, on dolerite. This rock is slightly orange, and by comparison with the rugged rhyolite of the rest of Snowdonia, slightly smooth. That forming the foot of the ridge is interestingly pimpled, improving the grip a bit. The ridge ascends in fine style to the summit trig point.

3. South flank As an alternative to the crest of the East Ridge, from the ridge foot a small path runs up left on Siabod's southern flank, on grass and occasional small boulderfields. It arrives on the summit plateau at a cairn 300 metres west of the trig point. Turn right, alongside a fence, and when the fence ends continue for 100 metres of rocky ground to the stone-built summit trig. You have reached it from the west, not from the east, and when it comes to leaving you'll need to double back along this same fence again.

---

4. Eastern cwm The ascent by the 'dolerite gates' is steep and the path is loose scree. But the scenery is special, as you ascend into the narrowing gap between two dolerite outcrops, to arrive a few steps from the summit trig. It's useful as a sheltered alternative when the east ridge is too windy, or as an uncomfortable but sheltered descent route.

From the small col before **Llyn y Foel**, fork right on a much smaller path. It contours around the base of the steep slope into the bottom of the eastern cwm. Here it turns uphill, zigzagging pleasantly at first but steepening to eroded scree. On either side are the dark crags of the east and the northeast ridge, with a jumbled rockfall below the former.

The path takes its inescapable line directly uphill, becoming slightly rocky as the crag walls close in at the very top. It arrives, quite suddenly, on the summit plateau, 100 metres northeast of **Moel Siabod**'s trig point.

Continuing from Moel Siabod: the summit pretends to be a rocky place, but down the back it's smooth grass. Descend west, with steep drops to left, after 100 metres finding and following the fence already used by those on Option 3 (the avoiding flank path ascent). The ground quickly changes from stones to smooth and comfortable grass, with paths either side of the fence. After 400 metres, a fence forks off left; cross the ladder stile if necessary and follow this forking fence, still west. It crosses the low but rocky hummock **Clogwyn Bwlch-y-maen** (though, oddly, the pass below is Bwlch Rhiw 'r Ychen). On this outing, the smallest hills have the biggest names, but this one

On Moel Siabod's easier northeast ridge, above Llynau Mymbyr

really is rocky. It's a dolerite sill, probably a continuation of the one that forms Siabod.

Enjoy the brief scramble, before the fence continues to a junction in the pass below. There cross a ladder stile and follow the continuing fence south up **Carnedd y Cribau**. At the top, grey rhyolite lavaflow is nicer to walk on than the dolerite was, and occasionally shows swirly patterns (flow banding).

From Carnedd y Cribau, the less nice stuff starts. Between the rocks and the bogs, it's pleasantly grassy. But you can't altogether avoid the bogs, nor the rocks either, so that often you find yourself knee-deep in the brown, or dropping over a sudden small scramble. The sketchy path follows the fence down southwest, with a small path, occasional ladder stiles inviting you to discover whether the other side of the fenceline is less swampy (it isn't). On the lower slopes you meet grey ashfall tuffs, then black basalt: both these are rocks escaped from the Snowdon eruptions.

After 1km, the fence turns down left, to pass below a crag outcrop; but it's better to stay above the crag, still southwest, for a grassy path that runs down directly to the ladder stile at the top of a crossing bridleway (SH666523).

A fairly good path continues to right of the fence, across another ladder stile, and into more swamps. Your legs start to drain again as you reach the rhyolite lava flow that forms **Cerrig Cochion**. The path follows the fenceline: at the highest point of the fence, divert up right for 50 metres through heather and rock to the summit cairn. There are at least three cairned summits but the one alongside the path is the highest.

Follow the fence onwards as it bends a little left. Two ladder stiles invite you to try the other side for a particularly swampy section before the path climbs through deep heather across the flank of **Moel Meirch**. A small cairn marks what may be the most convenient point to head up right, through heather, bilberry, and over rocks, to the complex top, which is a great place for games of hide-and-seek, particularly heart-stirring when in thick mist, very wet, and under an overweight rucksack. The rocks here are a depraved and exiled colony of the ashfall tuffs that form Y Lliwedd and the Idwal Slabs. The actual summit is at the northwest corner and is a rock pinnacle accessible by a short scramble from the northwest. On the final spike a single person can balance gingerly – certainly no room for the trig point the old OL map put up there.

Return to the path. Follow it and its fence past two little cols on the right to the corner of **Llyn Edno**. The path continues over the very small humps of **Ysgafell Wen**, **Moel Llynnau 'r-cwn** (669m), the **unnamed summit** (672m) and **Moel Druman**. Few of the forty-seven will be this easy.

A fence guides to the col 200 metres short of the summit of **Allt Fawr**. Here you glance down towards the urban dereliction of Blaenau Ffestiniog, thank the weather gods for any thick mist that prevents your actually having to see the place, then backtrack to **Llyn Conglog** to pass along its southern shore. Cross the outflow and continue straight ahead, ascending slightly, then dropping down a long shapeless ridge with steep slopes on the left and a small reservoir (**Llyn Cwm-corsiog**) ahead. Pass left of the reservoir, to pick up an old track at the corner of its dam.

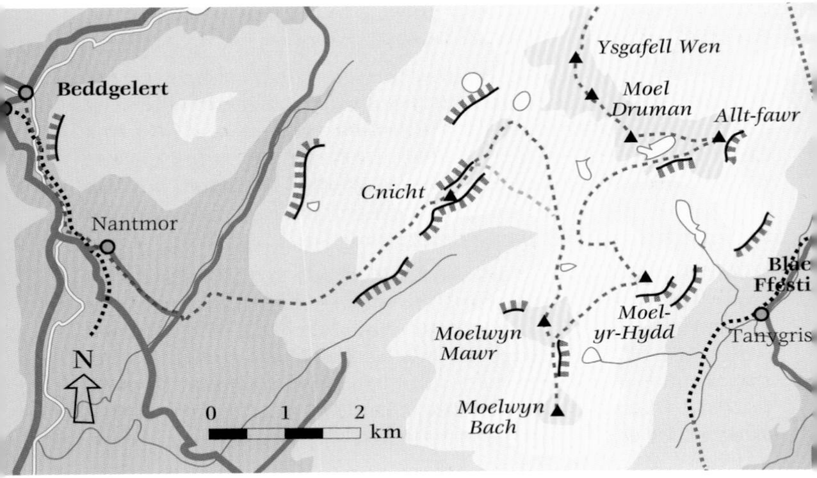

At the disused quarries at **Bwlch y Rosydd** (SH665462), quarrymen's cottages are crumbling elegantly back into the piles of slate they were made from. Here an incline leads south-east onto a flattish boggy area. Cross it eastwards onto **Foel Ddu**. It's a short walk south then up to **Moel-yr-hydd**.

Now descend west to the corner of a huge quarry hole, and pick up the path southwards (the lower of the two on the map). It's not yet time to climb Moelwyn Mawr, and this track traverses round its flank to Bwlch Stwlan, the col between it and Moelwyn Bach. This flank of Moelwyn Mawr is steep and broken but the path, built in stone terraces by helpful miners, is a treat no matter how unwieldy the sack. You look down across man-made levels and slate-tippings to the reservoir of Stwlan.

From **Bwlch Stwlan**, go up briefly to the foot of **Moelwyn Bach**'s rock snout. Now, round left, ignore a tempting terraced path contouring, but take the one that slants up across scree to approach the summit from due east. Take time, if necessary, to find this path: all other ways are appalling.

Back on Bwlch Stwlan, take the narrow rocky ridge of Craigysgafn to **Moelwyn Mawr**. After all the rough ground, Moelwyn Mawr's grassy dome is a place to lie down on and gaze back, across all the rocks and pools, to Moel Siabod; or to look anxiously forward to the hills beyond Beddgelert.

Descend northwards and pass to the right of Llyn Croesor to revisit those crumbling quarry buildings on their plateau of loose slates. Pick up the path northwards to the end of **Cnicht**'s east ridge (SH657477). Meanwhile pity the poor fellrunners who to save a couple of minutes are taking Cnicht's south face direct.

A bit of a Cnife-edge is Cnicht, with a serrated grey edge. It's a popular, well sat-on place, with cosy nooks to linger in and watch the sun go down across Tremadog Bay. The descent is long but gentle. You scramble down slightly left on a well-worn path, then take the grassy crest. At the 400m contour, a rocky rise is avoided on the right. Now waymarks start to appear, pointing to a grass track parallel to the crest but 100 metres down on the right.

Above Croesor (SH628451) more waymarks indicate the right turn onto the 'road used as public path'. It's a stony track, part of the Roman road Sarn Helen – though I wouldn't want to walk it myself in hobnailed sandals. After 1.5km (a mile) the track turns sharp left to slant down through trees to tarmac at **Bwlchgwernog**.

It's a shame to come off the hill onto the road? Well, this narrow one to Aberglaslyn is poor in traffic, but contrariwise rich in hill; its gradients will tax your end-of-day ankles.

scrambling on the southwest ridge of Cnicht

Nantmor's accommodation is limited: this gives you a chance to explore northwards towards Beddgelert. And if your bed should be Beddgelert, the exploring northwards is a treat. (The following section can start from either Aberglaslyn or Beddgelert.)

From the back corner of the car park, take the path left signed 'Aberglaslyn'. It rises to a junction where you fork left (away from the newly rebuilt railway) on a path through woods above the road. The path descends towards a kissing gate that would lead back onto the road beside the bridge over the big river. But turn right, away from this gate, onto the riverside path upstream.

This fisherman's path was once very rugged, but after the first stretch has been terraced and smoothed. It runs close above the river, soon with the railway emerging from its tunnels to run above. Below on your left, all the rainwater off the southern side of Snowdon – and that's a lot of rainwater – is running through a valley that's 50 metres wide. The craggy side-walls, the overhanging trees, the perched road, the narrow-gauge railway and even you: all seem uncomfortably squeezed and ready to fall into the river and get swept away.

After 1.5km (a mile) cross the footbridge beside the railway's one onto a concrete path. This runs towards **Beddgelert** along

the river's west bank. Beddgelert is the burying place of Prince Llewelyn's dog. The tomb of this mythic hillrunning animal is on the left just before the village.

Stage 5 EIFIONYDD

Beddgelert to Rhyd-Ddu

9½ miles (15.5km) height gain: 5300ft (1600m)

This is the group with only one easy hill. The single contourring of Mynydd-y-Ddwy-elor takes less time to walk over than to say. But Hebog is cruel and steep: before it, Bryn Banog is just as steep and covered with bracken. Moel Ogof and Moel Lefn have crags to find your way around, or to fall over, while Y Gyrn is some stuff that slopped out of the skip when they were taking the rubbish away to dump it on the Rhinogs. (Those of us who think the Rhinogs are wonderful will enjoy Y Gyrn and wish there was more of it.) But the end repays all. Mynydd Drws-y-coed is the most exciting high ridge of the Round; it makes you not mind at all missing out Crib Goch.

The ascent of Bryn Banog is pretty much pathless wherever you take it from. But from Aberglaslyn is the more awkward. (Bryn Banog, unnamed on most maps, is 519m high, 2km southeast of Moel Hebog.)

---

1. **Aberglaslyn to Bryn Banog:** This route up Bryn Banog is little used and obscure. But if followed with care, necessary paths do exist for all but one short section.

Cross the **Afon Glaslyn** and turn south on the A498 for 200 metres. Just above the driveway of Aberglaslyn Hall, a path slants uphill. Ignore a green arrow pointing right, and cross a footbridge on the main path. A stile on the left is marked 'private', and then a gate on the left is too. At this gate the path zigs sharp right. In another 50 metres, zag back sharp left on an eroded old walled path. It zigzags up to a stile at the top of the wood. (SH 5904 4602 – a lean-to shelter is nearby on the right here.)

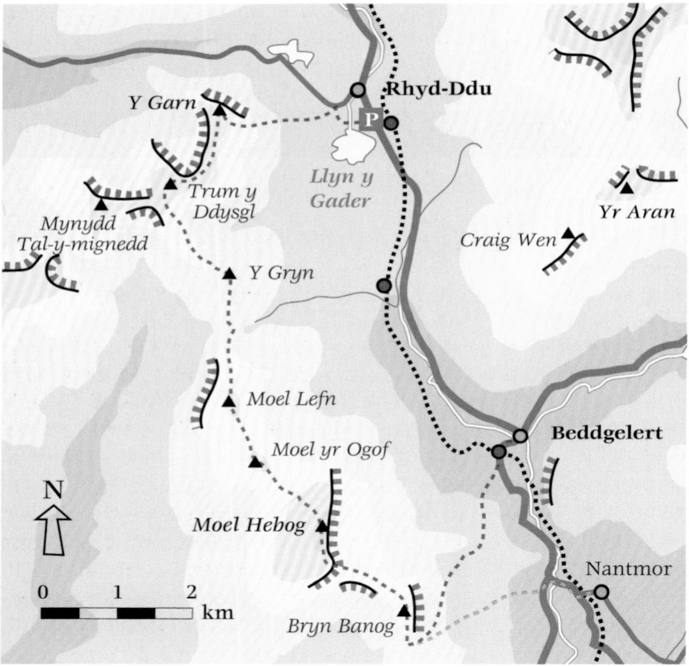

Head up to the right, west, to meet the stream on the right at the top corner of conifer plantations. Now you must move away from the stream again to avoid stone enclosures. So bear left, southwest, across wet ground, to a cairn at the bottom left corner of the stone walls (SH 5876 4586). Head uphill on a bracken path with a wall on your right to a wall gap (SH 5870 4578). Go through this on a cow path, and head to right of a ruined building to cross the next wall alongside the stream.

The next 200 metres are pathless, through an area where rhododendron has been eradicated, so the ecology may be still adjusting itself. Head up beside the stream for 100 metres, to where a bridleway track runs across the slope (on your right, it passes through a wall by a metal gate). Cross the bridleway and head up to left of the wall through rhododendron corpses. (They were once copses but they've been sprayed so now they're corpses.) Soon a small path forms. Follow it, with the wall always on your right, for 1km uphill. On the right, another wall with ladder stile arrives at the opposite side of the wall. Just above this, watch out for a stile of stone slabs through the wall, and clamber over it (SH 5790 4532). This leads onto open hill below **Bryn Banog**.

That open hill is, as already mentioned, steep. You could follow a faint path alongside the uphill wall to its high point, then turn up right alongside a broken wall. Or else just go straight up.

---

2. **Beddgelert to Bryn Banog**: Having diverted to Beddgelert, you may be tempted by the well used path up the northeast ridge of Moel Hebog. But that would miss Bryn Banog. To reach this outlier there is a direct route on an obscure bridleway.

Leave Beddgelert past the Royal Goat Hotel on the A498. After 300 metres, pass under the railway to a gateway on the right and a level crossing. With a graveyard on your right, take a small gate up on the left. Ignore a green arrow downhill and bear up right on a faint path into trees. Ignore a duckboard path on the left and head uphill to a gate, and a wall gap above it. Continue uphill, south, on very faint path traces, to a gate onto open bracken slopes (SH586474).

The bridleway path onwards is visible only occasionally. Weave among bracken patches uphill, still south. Once above the woodland on the left, the path slants left around a hill spur and past a ruin. Still slanting uphill it reaches a gate in a high stone wall (SH585466).

Ahead now lies the high open valley of **Afon Goch**, a place that's surely been pasturing cattle since they were domesticated in the Iron Age. And with no view of the world below, you could still be in the Iron Age – apart from the modern conformation of that beefy continental bull, and your own bright gaiters and strident jacket.

Cross the floor of the shallow valley; if you pass two gables of a ruined shieling (summer pasture house, or *hafod*) you may find the old path slanting uphill behind it. Whether you do or not, slant gradually uphill, southwest, to join a contouring wall above. Where this joins an uphill wall, it has a ladder stile (SH 5787 4528). Cross this and head straight up **Bryn Banog** above.

Continuing from Bryn Banog: A pleasant horizontal ridge leads northwards. Here you can forget the steep climb behind in the contemplation of the steep and rather rocky face of Moel Hebog ahead. To reach it, turn west at the ridge end to cross a boggy and confusing col. The face of **Moel Hebog** goes surprisingly easily up the green hollow of a small stream.

Hebog was the hard work: ahead lie two smaller hills that are rocky and rewarding. Descend from Hebog northwest; the slope is steep but grassy, and there's a wall and a comfortable bit of path. From the col follow the fence – if you dare – into a remarkable little chasm. There's no need to worry: if dragons do lurk here, they can only be very small ones as there's not much room. (Or make a way up to right of the chasm.) Rocky ground leads on to **Moel yr Ogof**. The brief descent to the col beyond may need a compass bearing in mist, as there's no clear ridge-line or path.

A direct northward descent off **Moel Lefn** would lead to crags. Take time to find the small path that winds down leftward to rejoin the crest for the flatter section around 500m altitude. As the ridge prepares to steepen again, drop right to the forest corner.

The 450m bump just ahead is **Y Gyrn**. A path circumvents it to the west, but it's one of the forty-seven Buckley ones, the fifty-three of this trip. Though it may not look much from here, from the valley below it's a fine spike on the horizon that you'd be sorry to have missed. A stone wall leads up through the deep heather: it's easiest just to right of the wall. Keep to rock tops rather than undergrowth where possible. From the summit descend northwest to rejoin the wall. It's grass again once you get to **Bwlch-y-Ddwy-elor**.

The final ridges are exposed enough that, in really high wind with a really large sack, it's wiser to avoid them. In which case take, with bitter regrets, the bridleway northeast from Bwlch-y-Ddwy-elor. A stile at the col leads into forest.

Follow the fence to the minor hump of Mynydd-y-Ddwy-elor (466m), then stroll the long gentle grass ridge above. It's got a shock at the top. The grass stops – just like that – and you're peering down into the deep hole of the Nantlle valley. For here the glacier has carried out one of its terribly simple effects, chopping off half the mountain and carrying it away into the Irish Sea.

Across the deep hole, the sunny cliffs of Craig y Bera smile back at you. Just a couple of wing beats away for a Nantlle raven, they're 600m down and up again on vertical grass both ways and out of reach of this particular long-distance expedition.

At **Trum y Ddysgl** it takes a moment to adjust to the way everything's suddenly gone vertical, and to discover that if you head off over the brink eastward you don't slide screaming into the northern corries but find, a few metres down the curve of oblivion, a sharp ridge springing out of the side of the mountain. There's a small path, and no actual rock climbing, and mostly you're a few feet down on the southern side of the crest. That's the side that isn't altogether vertical.

You won't want to be on this next col when it's windy. On a calm day, though, it's a place of rare perfection: a strip of narrow grass between green chasms, and overlooked by a sheer corner of Mynydd Drws-y-coed.

Mynydd Drws-y-coed has no cairn – a cairn might finally overbalance the mountain and send it toppling into the Nantlle valley. The nervous path stays a few feet below the highest point, on the southern slope. More rock-and-grass ridge-work leads on eastwards, with a little downhill scrambling at one point.

Y Garn is wider. Y Garn has room to move around and examine the huge and ancient cairns, but it's still the end of everything. Peer over the stone wall and you're suddenly looking down at 500ft (150m) of nothing with Rhyd-ddu at the bottom. Only the narrow neck of land behind you connects Y Garn to anything at all; do the cairns contain the bones of thousands who have arrived here and never found any way off?

Off is in fact possible. Grass slopes lead south-east then south, with a rough path keeping to the right of considerable craggy bits. Below a fence with ladder stile at 270m, the path runs down to a ladder stile into fields. A wide path leads down to a small gate and northeast to a corner of the B4418 (SH566526).

Without joining the road take a track on the right. After 200 metres keep ahead on a path marked with white arrows on rocks, to a footbridge. A slate-slabbed path over fields leads to the **Rhyd-ddu** station car park at the southeast end of its village.

As well as the sparkling Llyn y Gader to look at Snowdon over, Rhyd-ddu has a useful pub, bunkhouse and campsite, a bus stop, and a very slow but very scenic rail link to Caernarvon.

Gelert, faithful (but fictitious) hound

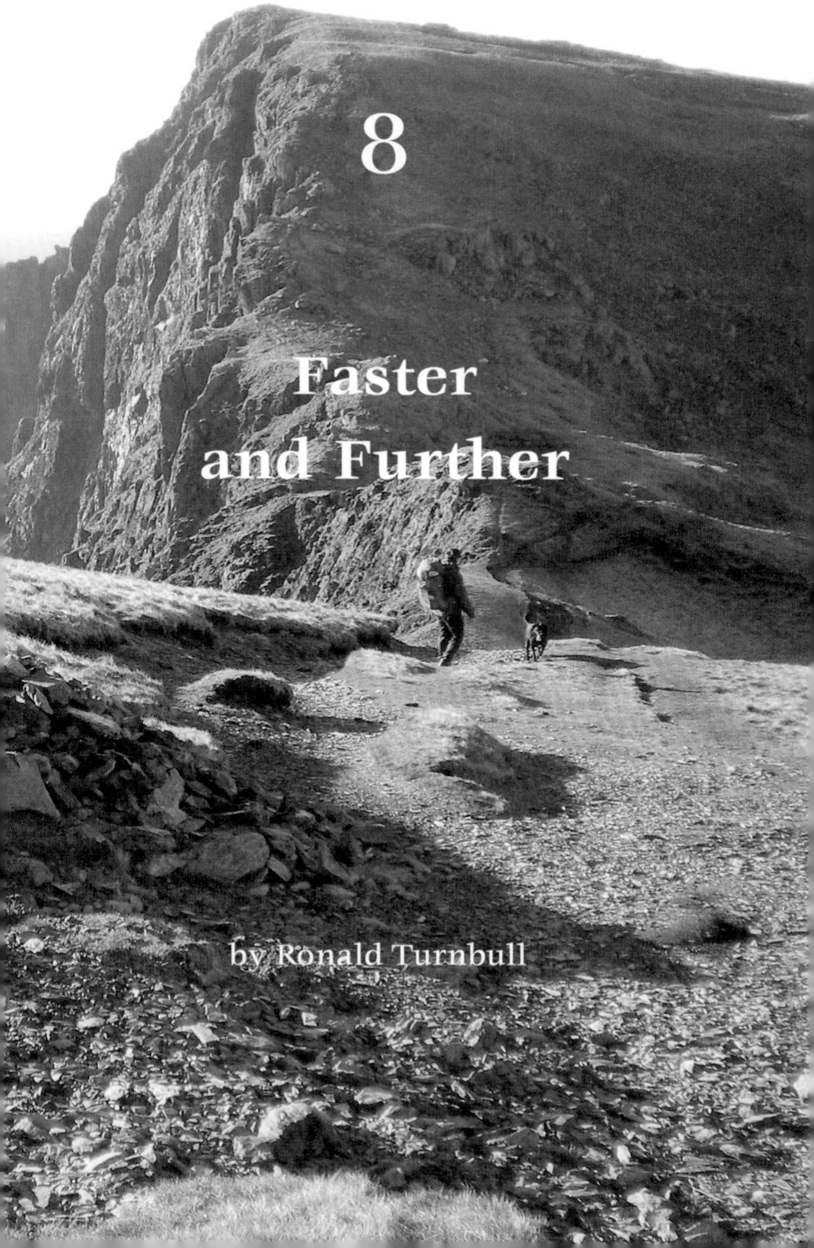

8

Faster and Further

by Ronald Turnbull

The Meirionnydd Round and other Monsters

The Snowdonia round – is it really quite as nasty as it could be? There are, after all, paths almost all the way. And anyone can enjoy a sharp rocky ridge, high above the cragged slopes of Llanberis or Cwm Idwal. OK, so the Buckley Round does have some rough county, and swampy stuff, and thigh-high heather, but is that 20 mile stretch along the northern Moelwyns really ruggedness enough?

It may have been such thinking, or it may just have been the realisation that Mark Hartell in 18 hours 10 minutes was going to be really, really difficult to beat. Either way, the answer is to run 70 miles, and over an improbable number of summits, somewhere slightly further south.

The first running of the Meirionnydd Round, over 23 hrs and 32 mins in 1998, won the 53 year old Yiannis Tridimas the Fell Running Association's Long-distance trophy for that year. So far, there has not been a second running of it. So there seems little point in calculating out the ideal schedule and pointing out how far apart are the resupply points. Briefly (insofar as anything about this over-excited bit of hillrunning can be considered brief) it starts at the base of Cadair Idris, and keeps going for 115km (72 miles) and 7200m (24,000ft) of ascent. But actually, it's not as easy as that sounds, because of the extreme roughness of much of the ground.

This dreadful circuit crosses 47 peaks of the Arans, Cadair Idris, Rhinog and Arenig. Of the 47 summits, some in the Rhinogs are pretty insignificant when you see them on the map. On the ground, of course, nothing in the Rhinogs is insignificant, not even Garn Gorllwyn (265m). Afterwards, the vigorous Tridimas realised he should have included Maen Du (Maesglase) a steep-sided craggy beauty at the head of the Dovey Valley.

To start, Cadair Idris could lull you into thinking this round was just more of the Snowdonian same. Cadair is a wonderful rocky mountain, with narrow ridges, huge crags, and twice as many corrie lakes as Snowdon itself. And once across the footbridge over the Barmouth sands, the southern end of the Rhinog country, while pathless, is pleasantly grassy. All that

Previous page: descending from Cadair Idris summit towards Craig Cau

comfortable stuff comes to a sudden stop after the round's sixteenth peak, Y Llethr. Suddenly, you're in the unique ruggedness of the real Rhinog, half made of rough grey gritstone and the other half of heathery holes.

Drag your limp legs, your scratched and bleeding ankles, out of the gritstone at Trawsfynydd with its disused nuclear power station. What's next? The country called Migneint and Arenig is a striking contest. Instead of bare rough rocks, there's bog and grassy tussocks. Instead of a hard-to-find 'cairn 518m' or 'knoll grid ref', small pointy hills can be seen for miles ahead as they emerge out of the bog and rise briskly into the grey clouds above. The prize here is Dduallt, pronounced slightly like 'thwacked', a hill that defends itself in depth. First there's a couple of kilometres of plantations, ringing it around like the Sleeping Beauty in her castle. Then there's a moat of mud. And having shown yourself worthy by getting past all that, Dduallt rises before you in steep, black, vegetated rock tiers. After another forest interlude, there's Rhobell Fawr, which is a sort of flattened Dduallt.

Just supposing you've survived all that, there's actually some nice running to round off the Round. The Arans are grassy-topped, but rendered exciting by the high sudden edge

Descending from the north top of Arenig Fawr with the south top ahead

that drops on the left-hand side. However, if what you really wanted in the first place was such runnable grassland with the sudden escarpment for excitement, then you should have taken yourself down to South Wales, where there's a continuous fifty miles of it...

The peaks, with Tridimas' times over them
Cadair Idris
Gau Graig (683m); Mynydd Moel (863m); Penygadair (893m); Cyfrwy (811m); Tyrrau Mawr (661m); Craig-y-llyn (622m); Braich Ddu (546m) **2hr 35min**
Rhinog
Garn Gorllwyn (265m); knoll 622183 (462m); cairn 623195 (517m); pillar 631210 (589m); Diffwys west top (642m); Diffyws (750m); cairn 667238 (688m); Crib-y-rhiw (670m); Y Llethr (756m); Rhinog Fach (712m); Rhinog Fawr (720m); cairn 663306 (518m); Craig Wion (566m); Clip (596m); Craig Ddrwg (596m); top 656337 (594m); top 657342 (578m); Moel Ysgyfarnogod (623m); Foel Penolau (614m); Moel y Gyrafolen (535m); Craig y Gwynt (431m) **7hr**
Migneint
Foel Fawr (528m); Graig Wen (556m); Carnedd Iago (535m); Arenig Fach (689m) **3hr 22min**
Arenig
Arenig Fawr (854m); Arenig Fawr south top (836m); Moel Llyfnant (751m); Dduallt (662m); Rhobell Fawr (734m) **4hr 49min**
Aran
Aran Benllyn (885m); Erw y Ddafad-ddu (872m); Aran Fawddwy (905m); Drws Bach monument (765m); Gwaun y Llwyni (685m); Glasgwm (780m); Pen y Brynfforchog (685m) **3hr 40min**
Dyfi Forest
boundary stone 794152 (659m); Waun-oer (670m); Mynydd Ceiswyn (605m) **1hr 46min**
total time, including 4 rests of 5 mins, **23 hrs 32 min**

The South Wales Traverse

In the south of Wales, the hills of the Brecon Beacon National Park are about as different from Snowdonia as can be. Snowdonia is a crumpled lump of volcanic rocks, grey-green to purple, with ridges running in all directions. The hills of south Wales are a simple straight line, made of sandstone. The sandstone is tilted up slightly to the north, to form a reddish, layered, line of cliff some fifty miles long. At just a couple of points the escarpment drops below 600m or 2000ft, plus one big hole where the River Usk breaks through. And at its highest, Pen y Fan of the Brecon Beacons comes within 94ft or 28m of being the sixteenth, and highly inconvenient, Welsh 3000-er.

The sandstone is a couple of geological ages younger than Snowdonia's volcanic rocks: it actually consists of rubble and dirt washed out from that continental mountain range as it eroded away over the following 50 million years. On the very summit of Pen y Fan, indeed, you can see ripple-marks in the sandstone where it formed at the bottom of a gritty lake. So these rocks, quite different from Snowdonia, are also quite a bit younger. This still doesn't make them young: by the standards of the rest of England, anyway, they are old. They are, as anybody can see, red. And that's why they call this stuff the Old Red Sandstone.

This gritty rock is quite soft and weathers round-edged. It is no good for climbing or even scrambling. What it is good for is walking, along that great north-facing escarpment, on the wide smooth paths or on the short-cropped grass, whose green appears almost lurid above the pinkish rocks. And what it's even better for is running, on and on along the ridgeline, on the gentle easy ground.

While this obvious high line has recently attracted a long high trail, the Beacons Way, that route does have continually to dodge down into the valley for food and a comfy bed to sleep in. Runners, though, don't need any of that. 50 miles, or even 75 (so as to take in every single summit of 2000ft or over) can be done non-stop, within a single day and night. And as for food, runners always know other runners whose knees are damaged or who don't feel quite as energetic as they are sometimes, and are willing to drive up and down the mountain roads bringing muesli bars, jammy sandwiches, and potent purple energy drinks onto the high ridgeline.

The South Wales Traverse has been run along since 1986, when Phil Dixon recorded 18 hr 10 min for the 120km with 5000m of ascent, and the 31 summits. Currently the record is held by Mark Hartell, who ran the long ridge in 14 hours 42 minutes in 1993.

The South Wales Travaerse **Start:** A4069 above Brynamman
Mynydd Du
Garreg Lwyd (616m); Garreg Las (635m); Bannau Sir Gaer (749m); Fan Brycheiniog (802m); Fan Hir (761m)
Fforest Fawr
Fan Gyhirych (725m); Fan Nedd (663m); Fan Llia (632m); Fan Frynych (629m); Craig Cerrig-gleisiad (629m); Fan Fawr (734m)
Brecon Beacons
Y Gyrn (619m); Duwynt (824m); Corn Du (873m); Pen y Fan (886m); Cribyn (795m); Waun Rydd (769m); Allt Lwyd (654m); Cefn yr Ystrad (Carn Felen) (617m)
Black Mountains
Pen Cerrig-calch (701m); Pen Allt-mawr (719m); Mynydd Llysiau (662m); Waun Fach (811m); Pen y Gadair Fawr (800m); Pen Twyn Mawr (658m); Chwarel y Fan (679m); Rhos Dirion (713m); Lord Hereford's Knob (690m); Hay Bluff (677m); Black Mountain (703m); Pen y Garn Fawr (616m)
Finish: Llantony Priory

All of the 2000ft (610m) summits of South Wales are included. What's a summit is arbitrary, and the runners count in the very minor hump of Duwynt, while skirting Fan y Big, a commanding peak right on the northern scarp with 30m (100ft) of drop round. The South Wales Traverse is 22km (14 miles) longer than the Paddy Buckley round, but with not much more than half the ascent and with much easier ground.

Sandstone cliffs of Carmarthan Fan

While it is relentlessly undulating, it doesn't have the very long ascents found in Snowdonia. One continuous ascent of 600m is considerably more tiring than two separate ones of 300m each – and the Traverse has only one 600m climb, onto the Black Mountains from the River Usk. Dishearteningly, the only 300m one is onto the outlier immediately before, Cefn yr Ystrad. A second inconvenient outlier beside the Usk, Mynydd Troed, falls just 1m short of the crucial 610m or 2000ft. Happy chance – or should we suspect a hillrunner with a shovel?

The limestone ground at the start of the run is pleasantly grassy, especially if you cleverly manage to avoid the occasional stonefields. The long sandstone ridge is simply a runner's dream - perhaps becoming even more so after 20 hours non-stop, as the hallucinations start to set in. There are plenty of road crossing points where your friends can wait with the excitingly purple-coloured drinks. The end result is that the South Wales Traverse takes about 3–4hr less than the Buckley Round, and 2–3hr less than Lakeland's Bob Graham Round. Any fit runner who starts slowly, eats and drinks, doesn't get lost, and avoids really nasty weather, certainly ought to have ten minutes to spare for the diversion over Fan y Big.

Cadair Idris, high point of Day 3 of the Dragon's Back Race

The Dragon's Back Race

Fifty miles a day, day after day, with the Parachute Regiment carrying the tent: this, we must suppose, is a foretaste of what awaits the dedicated hillrunner in the afterlife. Enter Wales at the top end. Sleep all night, eat large military meals, and run all day, following roughly John Gillham's *Snowdonia to Gower* long-distance route. Emerge five days later somewhere near Swansea. There would be the cream of British fell running, as well as eminent guests from abroad. There would be television cameras. There would be a bus to the station afterwards.

There was one thing I didn't ask myself. Does the Dragon's Back Race represent the ultimate reward of the well-behaved hillrunner – or of the wicked one?

Day 1: Carneddau, Glyders and Snowdon

The time was in the ancient days of 1992, when adventure racing had yet to be invented. The Dragon's Back had all the romance of a real adventure race, but without many of the features today considered essential, such as a hefty entry fee and lurid slick clothing paid for by the sponsor. No camera-friendly interludes of canoeing, hang-gliding, and underwater bungee jumping. But we did have the cameras. And the lazy 9am start the cameras called for meant the first day's race route had been rationalised to include only ten of the fifteen Welsh 3000s.

Glyn and I are strong, but slow. We left Conwy at the back, just in front of the motorcycle escort. But the Carneddau were cloudy, and effortlessly we overtook more serious runners, less serious hill-men, as they peeled off along incorrect ridgelines.

At 1:30pm we crossed the A5 onto Tryfan's North Ridge. We balanced across the tops of rock climbs, their final pitches rising out of the mist. At the summit, we were fifth last. This wasn't us overtaking, it was more people in front getting lost. Two German runners were calling like lost souls out of the summit clouds.

Four-twenty at Pen y Pass, and runners in proper lightweight gear can enjoy the wind and rain. So can runners like us in washed-out tee-shirts and nylon waterproofs. And when you're already leaping around on a high ridge with hardly any clothes on, vigorous gusts of wind just make it more exciting.

We arrived off Snowdon at 7 pm – eighteenth, after 10 hours on the hill. Our leg injuries, so far, were insignificant: just one twisted ankle, and that on one of Glyn's legs not mine. The leading pair of Martin Stone and Helen Diamantides had taken just under seven hours: now that's fell running.

Day 2: Moelwyns and Rhinogs

At the start they said, "Anyone want this midfield runner, lost his partner?" Perhaps unwisely, I said yes. In fact Stefan from Frankfurt didn't lose his partner. His partner dumped him after his poor performance on Tryfan. Stefan is very good on the roads and paths, but once up in the grassy rocky valley with the waterfalls and the croaking ravens, he turned out to be wearing unsuitable shoes. Soon enough we were back in the clouds, and then coming off Moelwyn Bach by a really terrible route, clambering down all the little cliffs. At one point Glyn abseiled down a tree root.

Bwlch Drws Ardudwy divides the Rhinogs.

The next bit cheered everybody up. It's a man-made surface, which reminded Stefan how good he is on the roads. That surface, however, is tilted sharply upwards, and goes among rough heather and rougher boulderfields, and the men who made it are referred to as 'Romans' though probably 17th-century Welsh.

Quite quickly we were through the pass, and onto the real Rhinog. The real Rhinog is jammed grey gritstone. Stefan became cragbound. "Nein es geht nicht, es ist gefahrlich zu Lebens," he said in his fluent German. "Niemand ist hier gesterben," I reassured him in my broken German. Nobody dies hereabouts. "Niemand?" "Ist Wahrheit."

As dusk thickened into full dark we got to the big green tents. We were on our legs for 13 1/2 hrs today. Stone and Diamantides took just 8 1/4 hours.

Day 3: Cadair Idris, Tarrens, Plynlimon

We strode up Cadair Idris's Pony Track. At the top was another windy rocky ridge with views of mist-filled emptiness.

Smooth grass that's tilted fairly steeply downhill can make you feel like a member of the Parachute Regiment yourself, but Stefan didn't appreciate it, and neither on this occasion did

Glyn. First Glyn's shoes had gone, and then that ankle again, and a thigh. We took three hours over Cadair Idris and were last but two; but still moving, in which respect we were doing better than many on this unprecedented hill race.

And the glamour and expense, the bright orange performance fabrics, of modern adventure racing – are they all a big mistake? The camera seemed to think so, as it lovingly filmed Glyn's collapsed shoes running through a puddle.

The Tarrens are rounded grassy hills with plantations creeping up the sides, overwhelming the very ridge. What was I doing on these Tarrens? I've got better hills at home in the Southern Uplands.

At Machynlleth, it was 3:15, and there were still fifteen miles to the top of Plynlimon. We were last. Over the next section race organiser Ian Waddell would act as escort and guardian angel. Glyn alternated walk and shamble and made quite strong progress, specially once we got off the road. This bit, that I'd expected to be a bore, went slowly but pleasantly. A grass road ran along the high moor, while on either side were deep valleys full of waterfalls, spruce, and green shadow. Much of the Southern Uplands has less to offer.

But at 6:15pm, at the track end under Plynlimon, the guardian angel told Glyn he must retire. Glyn knew that he could get over Plynlimon by nightfall, and even if he couldn't, he's got lots of experience of not getting over things before nightfall. He also knows that the race organiser's right even when he's wrong. Reluctantly, he climbed into the Landrover.

Stefan and I strode up Plynlimon in the last of the light. We got in at 8:10 without having to use torches. In other words, we didn't get benighted!

Day 4: Drygarn Fawr

The blisters came back up again in the night. Another 85 miles of slow jogging on blisters wasn't going to be altogether enjoyable but I decided to start anyway. I joined Glyn in the long queue for the Medical Sergeant. The Medical Sergeant gave Glyn's leg no more than ten miles, but he could start. So we did.

The well-wrapped blister became uncomfortable after the first mile but then didn't get any worse. A long trek along forest tracks led to seven miles of road. This middle bit of Wales sadly lacks mountains.

The way rose above vast oceans of industrial Birmingham's drinking water, on a stony path, a grassy path, and a high green lane between grown-out hedges.

Drygarn Fawr was only our second hill out of cloud, and a thoroughly dull one apart from two beehive cairns. But there's a nice way off, a little stream valley below the level of the moor. On the road through Abergwesyn my blisters started to boil out from under the bandage.

Day 5: Mynydd Du

The final day to Carreg Cennen Castle started with a long thirteen miles of country lanes. Just after the start Martin Stone and Helene Diamantides ran past with greetings – such a handsome couple. They had led the race for the first three days, but the flat fourth day had allowed Belton and McDermott to seize the lead by just four minutes. Thus Belton and McDermott had started this final day, with us, at 6am: Stone and Diamantides at 6:04, and anyone else with real chance of catching B and M at the appropriate time behind.

The lanes eventually led to the impressive scarp of' Bannau Sir Gaer (Carmarthen Fan): old red sandstone and fresh grass. The grass and sandstone themselves had been denied us because the race might damage the path, but what had to be a red kite was soaring above the place, and the grass and sandstone looked good even from underneath. Below the red-and-green lay a lovely lake with an orange tent. Here we stopped to think things out.

The man from Channel Four told stirring tales of the front runners, many hours ahead of us. Stone and Diamantides, a full seven minutes astray after the roads and tracks, took this slope direct, seizing back the lead in a short 750ft ascent. Great TV! "Not by chance," I told him. "All fixed up by Diamantides and Ian Waddell behind the food tent on Wednesday evening." He took a while to see the funny side of this joke.

We managed to enjoy a little hillrunning along the sandstone edge, then hobbled onwards into the limestone. It was nasty in bits: limestone boulder-fields are soapy-slippery but interesting, with sink-holes in the grass where underground caverns have collapsed. Down at Carreg Cennen castle they were filming runners as they climbed up out of the sunset – a special kink had been put into the route so that we should arrive eastwards. Meanwhile, we defied five separate leg injuries between the three of us by reaching the cairn of Tair Carn Uchaf.

We steered the two miles of path by torchlight and compass, searching each field-end for stile or waymark. The path changed direction nine times but Glyn's Celtic intuition, my compass and Stefan's torch got us through. It took a long time but it was fun. And so, at 9:00pm, we reached the castle. We'd finished. We weren't even last! We were 13th out of 17 pairs. But since 27 pairs started the race, 13th is actually in the first half of the field! We achieved our final climb, to the tall limestone castle set on its tall limestone rock, and got a brass dragon paperweight engraved 'survivor'. A Swede took notes on Glyn for his running magazine: "He has been in the pants for how long you say? Fourteen years?" We sat around appreciating our paperweights and telling one another about our injuries.

Next day Glyn, dissatisfied with this inland finish, hobbled off under his rucksack towards Swansea.

Martin Stone and Helen Diamantides, race winners, at Carreg Cennen Castle (photo: Nicola Gillham)

Manod Mawr, a 2000-footer east of Blaenau Ffestiniog, shows its attractive side. The rear of the hill, however, has been removed by quarrying.

The Welsh 2000s

In Spring of 1993, Ann Bowker realised that after 44 years constantly in the hills she really did have to consider herself as that exemplary being, the 'experienced walker'. So she set out to cross all the Welsh 2000ft summits in a single continuous walk.

There were many sound reasons for attempting such a walk. The linking of these hills, the Welsh equivalent of an all-the-Munros walk, had never been achieved by anyone of either gender. It would beat out a path for any solitary female walker, a snook cocked at our over-cautious and unnecessary alarmist age. It would raise money for a worthwhile charity.

In fact, only the second of these motives impelled her even slightly, and she was scornful in dismissal of the idea of charity sponsorship. If the walk was to be an unpleasant task motivated by money, then by what right was she to tramp 181 hills inflicting some damage to their fragile soggy turf? Whereas if it was an enjoyable project, why would her friends and admirers wish to sponsor it? Thus she concluded: "The most logical thing which I could do would be to be sponsored for every day I DON'T climb a hill and to give the money to a charity which is trying to preserve the wild areas of Britain!"

And in fact, enjoyment seems to have been her main, or only, motive for the walk. Ann Bowker has a serious talent for enjoying hills. Even in Spring, the least wet season, Wales provided plenty of rainfall: but Bowker enjoys a bit of rain. On Fan Fawr, Day Three, she takes particular pleasure in a sheltered brew-up: "Rain dripping from the rocks and the clammy sensation of damp clothing enhanced my enjoyment of the sweet hot coffee." Again: "Mist is just a different way of having fun on mountains". There's just one weather she does not have fun in: the thunderstorm. And she only had one of those, on Black Hill in the Black Mountains. (Which is, as it happens, the one Welsh 2000-er that's actually in England.)

Day after day she moved steadily over the exhilarating easy walking of the Old Red Sandstone, the big ridge that runs right across South Wales; the wet wilderness of Central Wales, where tall reeds whisper in the breeze below a grey sky and skylarks; the handsome crags of Cadair Idris; the tough, tough tramping of the Berwyns with their ankle-grabbing heather; the bare gritstone moorland of the Rhinogs, and the wonderful rocky ridges of Snowdonia.

The walk was almost unsupported: her camper van and husband met her just once along the way, on Day 17 at Milltir Cerrig pass in the Berwyns. In between times, she lived off the land: using pubs, youth hostels, shops and B&Bs as they arose. Many nights were spent in a small tent; not a few lying under the rain comforted by her one luxury, a lightweight radio with headphones. So, after a depressing weather forecast, she would lie listening to the raindrops on the nylon accompanied by one of the more melancholy late-romantic composers (Mahler, Bruckner). But on only two nights was she obliged to re-pitch the tent for a second successive night of being wet. At one point she almost ran out of gas cylinders but then found a helpful petrol station... Her account, which is on her website, has the same defect as those of John Hunt and Wilfred Noyce on Everest in 1953. It needs one or two disasters to make it more exciting.

It's quite surprising that this walk, as varied as the Scottish Munros but not so physically demanding and a more convenient distance, hasn't been copied many times. We can all, surely, spare one month out of a lifetime for a really long walk in Wales?

Ann Bowker's walk started on 6th April 1993 and took 35 days to cross the 181 summits then listed in the Nuttalls' *The Mountains of England and Wales*. 17 of the 34 nights were in the tent. The two days over Plynlimon were 'ghastly'. The most beautiful camp site was in the Rhinogs with the sun setting over Llyn Hwyel; the highest was near the summit of Carnedd Llewelyn.

The trip of approximately 600 miles, with 100,000ft of ascent, gave a daily average of 17 miles 2800ft (950km and 33,000m overall; 27km 950m daily average).

The Arenigs

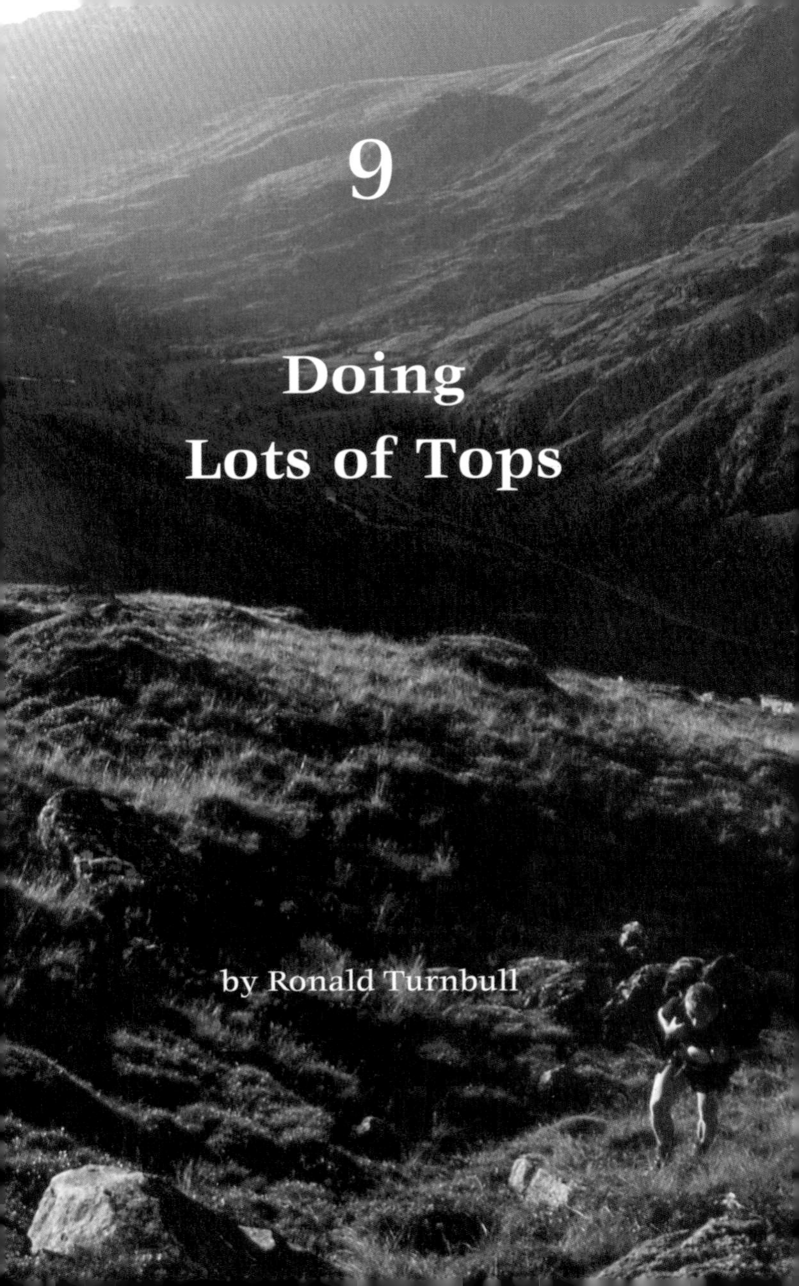

9

Doing Lots of Tops

by Ronald Turnbull

The Welsh 3000s: How to Run Them

If you're an athlete with serious intentions on Donnelly's record, all of what I write below will be useful to you except that you'll already know it. You should join the Eryri club, where you'll find the detailed advice, support and encouragement to clip those crucial minutes and seconds off the fifteen peaks. Donnelly himself was a member.

Lesser athletes will want to undertake the run just because it's such a good one. For them, the first runner's record, that of Thomas Firbank, might be a more realistic target. His time of 8 hrs 25 min (his wife Esmé achieved 9 hrs 29 on the same day) should be achievable, but not easily achievable. In its day it was a famous, even outrageous, run; and the account in *I Bought a Mountain* will have your PB trainers twitching out from under the cupboard.

If that's too slow for you, you could set your sights on Joss Naylor's time of 4 hrs 46. After all, even some of your friends who aren't runners have heard of Joss Naylor.

Direction: Snowdon is 143m higher than Foel-fras, so that the northbound direction is downhill. Against that we must set the fact that unpleasantly steep slopes cause less time disadvantage when taken in ascent. On the Welsh 3000s northbound, the main nasty downslope is off Pen yr Ole Wen; the one off Elidir Fawr is steep but grassy. Southbound, you have tricky rock-work off Crib Goch; the Llyn Glas variant reduces the steep stuff to 300m, which is why it's quicker. You also have Tryfan.

Record attempts have always started on Snowdon. By my reckoning, the extra 150m of ascent southbound costs 7.5 minutes: the reduction by 150m of nasty descent saves 3 minutes. If you're strong uphill but bad at coming down Tryfan, you might consider the backwards approach. Northbound has been the "official" direction; break the record backwards and cause some serious head scratching in the inner councils of the Fell Running Association.

Food: If you're unable to drink because of no appetite and no saliva, you're dehydrated. If you're unable to eat because of feeling sick, then you've been going too fast; the digestive system needs energy and your legs have used it all up. In either case the remedy is to slow down, and take a glucose drink (such as Staminade) in plenty of water. The ability to eat should return within half an hour.

If you're actually being sick, you've let things go too far. Stop, take the glucose, and spend ten minutes in some useful stationary activity such as taking photos or repairing your feet. A little more glucose, a mouthful of rice pudding, and continue slowly. With luck, new man (or woman) will kick in within half an hour.

The ideal menu is carbohydrate: slow-burning starch, plus a bit of instant-energy sugar. Popular foodstuffs are honey sandwiches, flapjack, rock buns, bananas, Mr Kipling's Bramley apple pies, custard, rice pudding, biscuits, muesli bars... perhaps not all at once.

A recent development is the powdered form of complex carbohydrate (starch) food such as Maxim, H5 or Isostar. These can be mixed with water and carried in a specially designed fuel tank between the shoulder blades. A plastic tube lets you sip at the stuff continually – maybe this makes you feel like an astronaut, maybe it makes you feel like a patient in intensive

Author Ronald Turnbull enjoys a bivvybag dawn on Snowdon at the end of a 3000s walk..

Previous page: Ascending Cwm Glas Mawr towards Crib Goch, summer evening

Tryfan, across Llyn Ogwen. On either the Welsh 3000s or the Buckley Round, some runners descend by a slanting line below the crags to reach the head of the lake, to ascend Pen yr Ole Wen by its east ridge. This variant suits those skilled in fast descents of rough strony ground.

care. Either way, a happy stomach means happy legs and more than repays the extra weight. (The same firms do glucose drinks, too, so you have to read the packets to work out which is which. Or you can mix them to create a powdered honey sandwich.)

Drink: Roy has carefully detailed the water sources; use them, every one. If it's hot, carry a small waterbottle in the bumbag.

Starting too fast: ensures that you stop having fun and start suffering rather early on in the run, and also end up finishing rather slowly. There are three ways to avoid:

Self-knowledge: if you can't chat to your companions, you're going too fast. If you can't eat in comfort, you're going too fast.

Schedule: the schedules in Section 10 are to help you go slow enough. If you're going even slower than the schedule, then stick the thing in your pocket and forget it. You're allowed to go faster than the schedule on the two descent sections; at the road breaks; and over the Carneddau. But elsewhere, stick to it.

Heart rate monitor: When you got the monitor, there was a piece of paper in the bottom of the box that blew away and got lost. This explained how to calculate your Aerobic Threshold, which is the heart rate at which you're using up oxygen faster than you can breathe. You want to get your heart rate to 80% of this level and keep it there. (On downhills and scrambling sections you won't be able to, though.)

Fitness: Ordinary training should be supplemented by endurance outings: trips over the hills of at least three hours. On the actual crossing you won't run uphill; it's quicker overall not to. But in training, run uphill. It hurts so much, it just has to be good for you.

Injury: Sprained ankles, and injuries to the ligaments and tendons of the leg, can be rendered bearable to run on with Ibuprofen or Aspirin. Stronger painkillers such as codeine are banned by the British Athletics Federation, to which the Fell Running Association is affiliated. They also affect the judgement, causing you to run over cliffs, into wrong valleys, snowstorms etc. Sprained ankles can be helped by dipping them in cold water for ten minutes. These measures treat the symptoms: running on when injured makes the injury worse and the sensible thing is to stop. But then, few really sensible people run hills.

Safety: The gear carried by the normal hillrunner (lightweight waterproofs, hat, gloves, thermal long johns and top) means that if the weather turns nasty, you only keep warm by keeping moving. If the weather turns nasty and then you injure yourself or get exhausted, then the Mountain Rescue will eventually find you but the anorexic chap with the scythe will probably get there first. So you either

- Carry more gear (e.g. proper survival bag) **or**
- Face death

Most hillrunners seem to go for the second option.

What you carry will depend on the weather, the weather forecast, how fat you are (skinny people get hypothermic sooner), whether you're running solo, and your personal risk/speed trade-off. The minimum that must be carried on long fell races in Britain is

- Waterproof trousers and top
- 2 oz high-calorie food

- map and compass
- whistle

Even with a support runner alongside, I'd carry that much. Support runners often drop behind and get abandoned.

Hypothermia and Heat-stroke: Which of these two you get depends if it's a cold day or a hot one. Hypothermia is made more likely by not eating enough, while heat-stroke is seriously bad dehydration. Both conditions can kill, and kill quite suddenly.

In either case the early symptom is tiredness – but you'll be feeling tired anyway, so may not notice. Later symptoms are irrationality, staggering gait, slurred speech and loss of judgement. "There's nothing wrong with my shpeesh," you'll say, while running round in circles in that snowstorm. Unconsciousness calls for urgent action by your support runner – awkward if you haven't got a support runner.

Supported or Solo? Failing reincarnation, solo lightweight hillrunning is as close as you'll ever get to being a bird. To stretch your legs across the smooth Carneddau at dawn when everyone else is asleep; to whizz down off Y Garn with wind in your hair and dip your sweaty head in the Llyn y Cwn; to drop like a loose boulder into Cwm Glas with a single boggy footfall every three yards; all this is very good. It is also rather risky. You're relying on your speed to keep you warm, your strong legs to get you off the hill.

If you know what you're doing, then do it. If you're not sure – perhaps you're a roadrunner who got fed up with running on roads, rather than a hillwalker who's speeded up – then find a support runner. Support runners are fun too, and warm friendships have been formed along these chilly ridges.

On the plateau of Glyder Fawr

Walking the Welsh 3000s

The technical advice for runners on the 3000s can also be consulted by walkers. Walkers just have to take all of my suggestions there a bit less seriously. For most walkers the aim will be to complete the walk within the day. The secondary aim will be to enjoy doing so – apart from the scree-climb to Glyder Fawr, it would be futile to attempt to enjoy that.

For those who seek to walk the fifteen peaks, four commandments are carved deep into the rocks of Snowdon.

Start early
Start slowly
Eat lots
Drink lots

For those who break even one of these commandments, special pains and torments await in the place appointed for such punishment: that place being roughly 300m above Idwal Cottage on the slopes of Pen yr Ole Wen.

Start early: Bivvy on Snowdon and you're bound to start early, you'll be too cold to lie around. But even if you sleep at sea-level, get onto the Pig Track before dawn. You'll find that uphill in the dark at daybreak is a very different game from downhill in the dark when you got benighted. Uphill in the dark's easier than downhill in the dark; your toes are unblistered; and you knew you were going to do it so you put fresh batteries in the torch. A quite unnecessary reward for such sensible behaviour comes with the looking down on the sleeping streetlights of Anglesey, the gleam of Llyn Llydaw under the moon, the final blaze of sunrise across Colwyn Bay.

Start slowly: Start slower than your usual speed. You're going to be tired at the end. Why start getting tired at the beginning?

Eat lots: To go twice as far as usual you need at least twice as much food. Take three lunches. Don't wait until you stop to eat. Fill your pockets with muesli bars, and practice in-flight refuelling.

Drink lots: Don't wait till you're thirsty – you're dehydrated long before that. Early dehydration and hunger are both mistaken by the ignorant brain for tiredness. Know better than your brain: eat, drink, and keep going.

Fitness: The most enjoyable way to get fit for hillwalking is to walk over hills. The time to do the Welsh 3000s is a fortnight after you finish ten days of intensive uphill stuff in Scotland or Lake District. If you want to train specially for your long walk, then exercise for 30 minutes, three times a week, for a month. The exercise should be vigorous enough to make you pant and sweat a bit. Strolling to work isn't enough unless you spend all day strolling to work. Jogging, cycling or swimming are convenient and effective.

Safety: Very tired walkers have trouble thinking straight. The Welsh 3000s are an unaccompanied walk only for those experienced walkers whose hillcraft is almost instinctive. Such will make their own decisions on what to leave behind in order to lighten the sack. I would carry:

a long-sleeved garment and a long-legged one, as well as
a lightweight waterproof top and bottom
hat & gloves
a survival bag
map, compass, whistle and torch
food (500gm: made up of sandwiches, Mars/Snickers, muesli bars)
a small water-bottle, for the Carneddau

Some sensible person should know what you're doing. Give them a specific time to call out the mountain rescue if they haven't heard from you. If you carry that survival bag, this specific time can reasonably be dawn the day after.

Running Paddy Buckley

The advice about starting slowly, eating lots, using the schedule and so on – all this applies to any attempt on the Paddy Buckley 24-hour circuit, but even more so. Start even more slowly, eat even more, etc.

The Buckley Round is that little bit more than the ordinary fit hillrunner can realistically hope to achieve in 24 hrs. Paddy

On the Gribin Ridge of Glyder Fawr

Buckley himself never quite managed it, and neither did I. Only make a serious attempt if you're more than averagely talented, very fit indeed, and totally familiar with the route. You'll probably already have done the Lake District's Bob Graham Round in around 22 hrs; this is a useful training run for the Buckley one.

If you are such a one as I describe, then I can only gaze in awe at your mighty calf-muscles, your far-away obsessive eyes, and marvel at the easy competence with which you handle the Camelbak food system and the electronic heart monitor.

About the Route

Three types of person attempt the Buckley Round. There are those who prepare by walking, or running, every step of the route beforehand, in thick mist if they can get it, making careful notes on fence junctions and the shapes of summit cairns. Others rely on map skills sharpened to perfection by the simple process of getting lost on Mountain Marathons. A third group just start running and hope for the best – a forlorn hope in a world where tops and even bottoms suddenly go away into clouds, fences sink into the bog and get rebuilt somewhere slightly different and even the OS 'Outdoor Leisure' map has mistakes on.

None of the three will benefit from a detailed step-by-step route guide given in the 5-day backpack of Section 7: the first two don't need it, and the third doesn't have time to read it, having lost half an hour already on the wrong summit of Moelwyn Bach.

This is not work for words. For this you use your map.

When your tent leaks in the middle of the night, you hunt out your moleskin plasters and see what you can do to patch over the holes. In the same spirit, the words below attempt to patch over a few small holes in the map

Secret summits			
These tops are not marked on Landranger or Outdoor Leisure maps			
19	Ysgafell Wen	SH664488	
20	Mynydd Llynau 'r Cwn	SH664485	669m
22	Unnamed summit	SH667481	672m
28	Craigysgafn	SH660445	
30	Bryn Banog	SH576457	519m
34	Y Gyrn	SH553501	
35	Mynydd-y-Ddwy-elor	SH549504	466m
41	Cribau Tregalan	SH605536	931m

1: Elidir Fach: Three bridges cross the Afon Rhythallt between the Llyns Padarn and Peris. The western one is a footbridge, served by a rough path. Then comes a railway, and the eastern one, beside Llyn Peris, is the bridge crossed by the motor road. From the road bridge the path suggested in 'Buckley: the Backpack' zigzags up between slates to the horizontal track at 200m altitude marked on the map as a public footpath. Buckley contenders have followed this railbed 100 metres east, then continued up the inclines, passing to left of a huge quarry hole to the very top of the quarries. This is blocked by fences and notices 'keep to public footpath'. For runners the quickest alternative is to head out of Llanberis southeast on the A4086 for 2km (1 1/2 miles) to take the right of way from the head of Llyn

Roy Clayton sets off northwards from Foel-fras

Peris. This is nastier, but quicker than the alternative route for walkers in Section 7.

Ogwen: For an alternative descent of Tryfan via the head of Llyn Ogwen, see Variation G3 on page 81, and the picture on page 178.

13: Pen Llithrig y Wrach: descent (and short cut for Buckley Backpack walkers): The obvious southward ridge leads to steep, deep, heather. It's better to head down southwest, slightly less steep and with grass but still some heather. At about 600m, join a fence running south, and then southeast.

At the foot of y Wrach's south ridge, the fence bends left, with a ladder stile (SH715608) that would lead to a bridge over a leat (artificial stream). Don't cross this stile, but head left along the fence for 200 metres to another leat bridge, a wide, metal one. Cross this onto a boggy path with an old fence alongside it. On either side the heather-tips practically tickle your chin: get lost here and you're in deep trouble – deep heather trouble.

The bridleway wanders off left of the leat, rejoining it after 300m to cross at a third footbridge. It continues gently down southwards, a wide grass path with occasional posts; a fence runs to left of it at first. Just after a ladder stile, the path forks, the left branch being more direct but the paths soon recombining to run leftwards to Tal-y-waun. Pass above the buildings, and cross a slanting track onto the pathline that slants down to reach the A5 at a ladder stile and footpath sign.

Walk down the road to Capel Curig's main road junction – there's a very narrow pavement.

14: Moel Siabod: Option 1, obviously. From the A4086, through the roofed entry of Plas y Brenin and up right to pass to right of a dry ski slope to a gate, is quicker for runners.

29: Cnicht: The right-of-way leading to the foot of the small reservoir Llyn Cwm-y-foel has no existence on the ground that I could detect. Nevertheless this is a satisfactory way to Cnicht, the intimidating southeast slope of which yields at this point, if trudged up with sufficient persistence.

30: Bryn Banog: The right-of-way from Aberglaslyn is lost under deep bracken. Send wide friends in advance to trample the way. If you have friends who happen to be cattle, they'll do a fine job for you.

Rhyd-ddu: The footpath running eastwards across the valley floor to the car park is worth seeking out.

Descent from Glyder Fawr towards Llyn y Cwn

10

Data Section

Colin Donnelly's Record Run			
11th June 1988: Start time 10:30 am			
Peak	Split Time min:sec	Time from Start hr	min:sec
SNOWDON			
Yr Wyddfa			0:00
Carnedd Ugain	4:56		4:56
Crib Goch	9:33		14:27
Blaen-y-nant	14:54		29:23
Nant Peris PO	7:32		36:50
THE GLYDERS			
Elidir Fawr	36:10	1	13:00
Y Garn	22:00	1	35:00
Glyder Fawr	19:00	1	54:00
Glyder Fach	9:18	2	03:18
Tryfan	16:42	2	20:00
Ogwen	13:00	2	33:00
THE CARNEDDAU			
Pen yr Ole Wen	38:00	3	11:00
Carnedd Dafydd	11:00	3	22:00
Yr Elen	20:00	3	42:00
Carnedd Llewelyn	12:00	3	54:00
Foel Grach	10:40	4	04:40
Carnedd Uchaf	6:04	4	10:44
Foel-fras	9:12	**4**	**19:56**
Pacers Don Williams, Emlyn Roberts, Del Davies, Huw Parry and Fon Williams **Sponsored by** Reebok			

Thomas Firbank, Eric Beard, Joss Naylor: each of them, on completing his record-breaking run, gave his opinion that the record could be improved on. And in each case, nobody else believed it possible. The same goes for Colin Donnelly's one, detailed above. Donnelly says he was too slow over the Carneddau, and that a *really* good runner could improve this time by 5 or 10 minutes. Everybody else thinks that's quite impossible.

The record has now stood for over 20 years. This time, the poeple who think it's unbreakable may actually be correct ...

The Welsh 3000s						Schedules			
	distance		ascent		Schedule J		Schedule F		
	mls	km	ft	m	min	ETA	min	ETA	
SNOWDON									
1 Yr Wyddfa						00:00		00:00	
2 Carnedd Ugain	0.5	0.8	200	50	5	00:05	9	00:09	
3 Crib Goch	0.9	1.4	200	50	19	00:24	32	00:41	
A4086 Blaen-y-nant	1.6	2.6			21	00:45	36	01:17	
Nant Peris	1.3	2.1			7	00:52	11	01:28	
Total	**4.3**	**6.9**	**400**	**100**	52 min		**1 hr 28**		
rest							10	01:38	
GLYDERAU									
4 Elidir Fawr	2.3	3.7	2700	800	43	01:35	72	02:50	
5 Y Garn	2.2	3.5	800	250	24	01:59	39	03:29	
6 Glyder Fawr	1.4	2.2	1000	300	20	02:19	33	04:02	
7 Glyder Fach	0.9	1.4	300	100	9	02:28	16	04:18	
8 Tryfan	1	1.6	600	200	18	02:46	31	04:49	
Ogwen	1.2	1.9			19	03:05	32	05:21	
Total	**9**	**14.4**	**5400**	**1600**	2 hr 13		**3 hr 43**		
rest							10	05:31	
CARNEDDAU									
9 Pen yr Ole Wen	1.1	1.8	2300	700	33	03:38	57	06:28	
10 Carnedd Dafydd	1	1.6	400	100	11	03:49	20	06:48	
11 Yr Elen	2.4	3.8	300	100	20	04:09	34	07:22	
12 Carnedd Llewelyn	0.9	1.4	600	200	13	04:22	22	07:44	
13 Foel Grach	1.1	1.8	100	30	9	04:31	15	07:59	
14 Garnedd Uchaf	0.7	1.1	100	30	6	04:37	10	08:09	
15 Foel-fras	1	1.6	200	50	9	04:46	16	08:25	
Total	**8.2**	**13.1**	**4000**	**1200**	1 hr 41		**2 hr 54**		
Welsh 3000s	**21.5**	**34.5**	**9800**	**3000**	**4 hr 46**		**8 hrs 25**		

In the table above, schedule J is calculated to equal the time of Joss Naylor, and Schedule F, of Thomas Firbank.

Notes

- Calculated schedules take account of distance and ascent, but also of rough ground and nasty descents. A slowing-down factor of 6% is included after Ogwen. Donnelly slowed down by 20%, confirming his suggestion of a poor finish over the Carneddau.
- Distances are measured off the map. For convenience of calculation they make no allowance for wiggles, distance up slope. For boasting purposes, 10% may be added.

Colin Donnelly at Foel-fras at the end of his record-breaking 3000s run

- Descents to Blaen-y-nant, Ogwen: descent-times vary widely with the skill of the descender. Donnelly, a demon descender, improved on calculated times by 25%.

Welsh 3000s: schedule for walkers	
up Snowdon	2 hr
Snowdon massif	2 hr
Glyders	6 hr
Carneddau	5 hr
Total Welsh 3000s	15 hr
off Foel-fras	1 hr
North to South walkers but add time for any scrambling on Tryfan and Bristly Ridge	
up Foel-fras	2 hr
Carneddau	4 hr
Glyders	6 hr
Snowdon massif	3 hr
Total Welsh 3000s	15 hr
off Snowdon	1 hr

The Paddy Buckley Round

Paddy Buckley's 24-hour Round may be run in either direction, and started at any point, and at any time of day or night. The choice of direction is determined by the amount of steep or difficult downhill. The anticlockwise direction would involve such descents off Pen yr Ole Wen, Tryfan, Glyder Fawr, Elidir Fawr, Cribau Tregalan, Moel Hebog, Cnicht and Craigysgafn. This direction is rarely attempted.

Given the clockwise direction, steep downhill again determines the choice of start-point. As you go round you go slower, but the effect of tiredness is most marked on tough descents: Tryfan tired takes 50 minutes instead of 30. Clockwise, the tough descent is Tryfan, with lesser bad bits off Glyder Fach, Yr Aran (Snowdon), and Pen Llithrig y Wrach. To get these in early, where they are less damaging, a start at Rhyd-ddu or Llanberis is suggested.

Darkness has little effect on road or uphill progress, considerable effect on horizontal boulderfields and most effect on those difficult descents. Tricky route finding over the rocks and bogs of the Siabod/Moelwyn group also asks for daylight. The Snowdon section is the one reasonably easy one underfoot; that and the following long ascent from Llanberis are the best stretch to do in the dark.

I prefer to have the night section early in the run. With the uncertainties of night still ahead, it's tempting to run faster than the schedule: and running too fast at the start is the commonest bad mistake. Darkness can actually be made to help you by preventing you from running too fast over an early, easy section.

Paddy Buckley Round Schedule

The following schedule is for Llanberis start at 1:00 am and clockwise circuit. The gray rows are the hours of darkness at midsummer.

Paddy Buckley Round		distance mls	km	ascent ft	m	time calc	min	ETA
1	**Glyders**							
	Llanberis							0100
1	Elidir Fach	1.8	2.9	2300	700	63	53	0153
2	Elidir Fawr	0.5	0.8	500	150	15	17	0210
3	Mynydd Perfedd	0.9	1.4	200	60	14	14	0224
4	Foel-goch	0.5	0.8	400	120	13	12	0236
5	Y Garn	1.2	1.9	600	180	25	22	0258
6	Glyder Fawr	1.4	2.2	1000	300	35	35	0333
7	Glyder Fach	0.9	1.4	300	100	16	16	0349
8	Tryfan	0.9	1.4	600	180	22	35	0424
	Ogwen	1.2	1.9			15	30	0454
	Total	**9.3**	**14.9**	**5900**	**1750**		**03:54**	
	rest						10	
2	**Carneddau**							
	Ogwen dep							0504
9	Pen yr Ole Wen	1.1	1.8	2300	700	55	56	0600
10	Carnedd Dafydd	0.9	1.4	400	120	18	16	0616
11	Carnedd Llewelyn	1.9	3.0	400	120	30	30	0646
12	Pen yr Helgi Du	1.3	2.1	400	120	23	26	0712
13	Pen Llithrig y Wrach	1.2	1.9	600	180	25	23	0735
	Plas y Brenin	3.1	5.9			37	37	0812
	Total	**9.5**	**15.2**	**4100**	**1250**		**03:08**	
	rest						10	
3	**Northern Moelwyns**							
	Plas y Brenin dep							0822
14	Moel Siabod	2.2	3.5	2300	700	68	58	0920
15	Clogwyn Bwlch-y-maen	1.7	2.7	100	30	22	18	0938
16	Carnedd y Gribau	0.5	0.8	200	60	10	10	0948
17	Cerrig Cochion	1.9	3.0	600	180	34	38	1026
18	Moel Meirch	0.5	0.8	400	120	13	14	1040
19	Ysgafell Wen	1	1.6	300	100	17	22	1102
20	Mynydd Llynnau'r Cwn	0.2	0.3	100	30	4	4	1106
21	Unnamed (672m)	0.4	0.6	100	30	7	7	1113
22	Moel Druman	0.5	0.8	200	60	10	10	1123
23	Allt-fawr	0.6	1.0	300	90	13	14	1137
	Bwlch Cwmorthin	1.1	1.8			14	18	1155
	Total	**10.6**	**17.0**	**4600**	**1400**		**03:33**	
	rest						10	

4	**Moelwyns & Cnicht**							
	Bwlch Cwmorthin dep							1205
24	Foel Ddu	0.4	0.6	500	150	15	15	1220
25	Moel-yr-hydd	0.3	0.5	300	100	10	9	1229
26	Moelwyn Bach	1.5	2.4	700	200	33	31	1300
27	Craigysgafn	0.5	0.8	300	100	12	13	1313
28	Moelwyn Mawr	0.4	0.6	300	100	11	10	1323
	Bwlch Cwmorthin (near)	1.1	1.8			14	14	1337
29	Cnicht	1.4	2.2	1000	300	38	38	1415
	Aberglaslyn	3.7	5.9			52	50	1505
	Total	**9.3**	**14.9**	**3300**	**1000**		**03:00**	
	rest						15	
5	**Eifionydd**							
	Aberglaslyn dep							1520
30	Bryn Banog	1.7	2.7	1700	500	55	50	1610
31	Moel Hebog	1.1	1.8	1100	350	36	34	1644
32	Moel yr Ogof	0.9	1.4	400	120	20	20	1704
33	Moel Lefn	0.4	0.6	200	60	9	12	1716
34	Y Gyrn	1.1	1.8	400	120	22	24	1740
35	Mynydd-y-ddwy-elor	0.4	0.6	200	60	9	12	1752
36	Trum y Ddysgl	0.9	1.4	800	250	27	27	1819
37	Mynydd Drws-y-coed	0.4	0.6	200	60	9	9	1828
38	Y Garn	0.5	0.8	100	30	8	12	1840
	Rhyd-ddu	1.4	2.2			18	26	1906
	Total	**8.8**	**14.1**	**5100**	**1500**		**03:46**	
	rest						15	
6	**Snowdon**							
	Rhyd-ddu dep							1921
39	Craig Wen	2.5	4	1400	400	64	57	2018
40	Yr Aran	0.6	1.0	600	180	21	19	2037
41	Cribau Tregalan	1.4	2.2	1400	400	49	55	2134
42	Yr Wyddfa (Snowdon)	0.6	1.0	600	180	21	18	2152
43	Carnedd Ugain	0.5	0.8	200	60	11	11	2203
44	Moel Cynghorion	2	3.2	600	180	41	49	2252
45	Foel Goch	1.2	1.9	500	150	27	23	2315
46	Foel Gron	0.5	0.8	400	120	15	16	2331
47	Moel Eilio	0.9	1.4	400	120	21	16	2347
	Llanberis	2.9	4.6			41	35	0022
	Total	**13.1**	**21.0**	**6100**	**1850**		**05:01**	
Paddy Buckley Round		**61ml**	**98km**		**8700m**		**23:22**	

The calculated timings are derived from Naismith's formula (80m up = 1km extra, or 1000 ft up = 1 mile extra) and speeds

7.5 min/km (12 mins/mile) over Glyders, Carneddau, Moelywns to (15) Clogwyn Bwlch-y-maen

8 min/km (13 min/mile) remaining Moelwyns, Eifionydd

8.75 min/km (14 min/mile) Snowdon Range

The scheduled time is adjusted to take into account the roughness of some terrain, and previous recorded times.

Daylight Hours and weather

Internet weather forecasts:
www.mwis.org.uk (currently Thur–Sat only)
www.metoffice.gov.uk/loutdoor/mountainsafety/
webcams:
Llyn Ogwen www.ogwen-rescue.org.uk/oggi_cam/
Snowdon from Elidir Fawr www.fhc.co.uk/cams.htm
see also www.bbc.co.uk/wales/northwest/sites/webcams
Summit panoramas: computer views from Snowdon, Glyder Fawr, Carnedd Llewelyn and a dozen others at www.viewfinderpanoramas.org

The table lists times of sunset and sunrise for Snowdonia. Dawn and dusk are, roughly, when it's possible to read a map by natural light. Useful light to walk or run by extends up to half an hour longer if skies are clear. All times are British Summer Time except March.

	Dawn	Sunrise	Sunset	Dusk
June 21	4:10	4:55	21:45	22:30
May 21, July 21	4:30	5:15	21:20	22:05
April 21, Aug 21	5:30	6:10	20:30	21:05
September 21	6:45	7:15	19:15	19:50
March 21 (GMT)	5:45	6:15	18:15	18:50

Overnight runners on the Buckley round will want to know about the moon as well as the sun. Dates of the full moon can be found in diaries and on calendars. On the days around the full moon, there will be useful light for the greater part of the night. Even with slight cloud cover, this light of the full moon can be enough to see your way by. (You still need the torch, though, to read the map with.)

During the week before the full moon, there is moonlight during the first part of the night only. During the week after full moon, moonlight is in the hours before dawn. During the week either side of the new moon, there is little useful moonlight.

Times of moonrise and moonset are in Whitaker's Almanack. Even small public libraries should have a copy. See also HM Nautical Almanac Office www.nao.rl.ac.uk and seek data for Latitude 53°00' North Longitude 4°00' West (which is near Cnicht) – or download data for Cambridge and add 16 minutes to them.

Bob Wightman's website, www.bobwightman.co.uk, has a Paddy Buckley Round calculator which generates a schedule including hours of darkness (but not moon).

Maps

For the Welsh 3000s, the Welsh 1000s and the Snowdon Horseshoe you can get by with the Landranger 1:50,000 No. 115 'Snowdon', but the double sided Explorer 1:25000 No. OL17 'Snowdon' is far superior for route finding as it shows fences and walls, and details many more of the crags. RT says it's a bit bulky and awkward to use for runners, though – he also finds the Harvey Superwalker map far easier to read on the Glyders and Tryfan.

On the Paddy Buckley Round you'll need in addition either the Explorer Map OL18 'Harlech & Bala' or the Landranger 124 'Dolgellau'. Note too that Explorer OL17 misses out Moel Siabod.

The excellent Harveys Superwalkers (1:25,000) 'Snowdon & Moelwynion' and 'Glyderau & Carneddau' cover the 3000s route and the Buckley Round (but not the start of the 1000m Peaks route). They're waterproof and will not disintegrate in the rain or snow, which is useful – but you'll have to carry two maps. The contour detail on Superwalkers is much clearer than on Explorers: this is a particular boon by torchlight or to those with fading eyesight or rain-dampened spectacles. The disadvantage of Superwalkers is that they mark fences and walls only on the hill, not in the valleys.

The recent Harveys Snowdonia Mountain Map covers the 3000s, the 1000m Peaks route, and the Buckley Round on one map at 1:40,000 scale. This very useful map could even be an emergency groundsheet as it's on tough waterproof plastic. Spectacle-wearers won't find it so clear and easy to read as the larger-scale Superwalker.

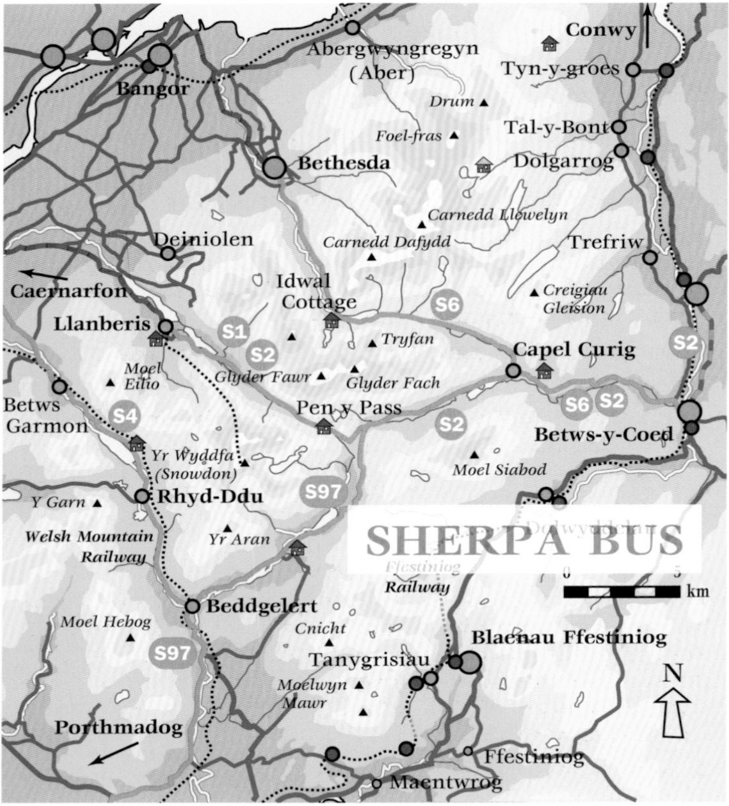

SNOWDON SHERPA BUS SERVICE
The times given below are approximate only, and for the Summer timetable. For current timetables, go to www.gwynedd.gov.uk
S1 Llanberis - Pen y Pass
The only service so far with a usable evening timetable. Summer timetable 8am (weekends) or 9.30am (weekdays) to 9pm, half-hourly (weekends) and hourly (weekdays) during peak times, daily. Llanberis - Nant Peris - Pen y Pass - Pen y Gwryd.
S2 Llanrwst - Betws-y-Coed - Capel Curig - Pen y Pass
Core service Betws - Pen y Pass 8am - 6pm, hourly
S4 Caernarfon - Snowdon Ranger - Rhyd-ddu - Beddgelert
Every 2 hours, 7.30am to 6pm from Caernarfon. Late bus back to Caernarfon 10pm. Fewer on Sundays.
S6 Bethesda - Llyn Ogwen - (Pen y Pass) - Capel Curig - Betws-y-Coed
Bethesda - Betws 5 a day 8am - 6pm. A couple are via Pen y Pass. Extends once a day to Caernarfon (but there are other buses Caernarfon - Bethesda)
S97 Porthmadog - Aberglaslyn - Beddgelert - Nant Gwynant - Pen y Pass - Capel Curig - Betws-y-Coed
Core service Beddgelert - Pen y Pass 2-hourly 9am - 5pm Mon - Sat. Only 3 a day on Sundays.

Transport

By Railway

1 North Wales coastal line via Llandudno calls at Bangor, with bus links via Caernarfon to the Sherpa buses to Llanberis and Rhyd-ddu. The branch line from Llandudno Junction runs to Betws-y-Coed, the other connection for Sherpa buses to Capel Curig. (From Pen y Pass and Beddgelert, the least slow Sherpa out could be to either Caernarfon or Betws.)

2 Mid Wales line to Porthmadog from Shrewsbury via Machynlleth

3 While we discreetly ignore the Snowdon Mountain Railway (oh all right then, www.snowdonrailway.co.uk 0844 4938120) the Welsh Highland Railway links the bottoms of various routes up and down Snowdon allowing complete crossings of the mountain. It has now reached Beddgelert and will eventually reach Porthmadog: www.festrail.co.uk 01766 516024

4 Ffestiniog Railway from Porthmadog into the Moelwyns, same contact details.

By Coach

National Express or Eurolines services from London, Birmingham, Liverpool, Manchester, Leeds to Bangor and Caernarfon: tel. 08717 818181 www.nationalexpress.com

Local Buses

The Snowdon Sherpa is reliable, friendly, and not too expensive. But the services are roughly every two hours, don't start early, and many stop at late afternoon. Most services connect at Pen y Pass.

Local bus timetables including the useful Snowdon Sherpa are at www.gwynedd.gov.uk (click 'public transport' then 'timetables' or 'journey planner'). Paper timetables can be obtained from National Park Office, Penrhyndeudraeth, Gwynedd LL48 6LF Tel. 01766 770274; or Bws Gwynedd ED, Gwynedd Council, Council Offices, Caernarfon, Gwynedd LL55 1SH Tel. 01286 672255. The Gwynedd paper timetable currently maps the Sherpa routes but does not give times for them. Those times are in the Conwy timetable, from Conwy County Borough Council, Public Transport Section, The Heath, Llanfairfechan LL33 0PF Tel. 01492 575412

Timetable enquiries, www.traveline-cymru.org.uk, Tel. 0871 200 22 33 or Bws Gwynedd 01286 679 535

A few years ago the 'Snowdonia Green Key' proposed seriously expensive parking within the mountains and a frequent, all-day Sherpa service from car parks at entry points like Llanberis. Neither hill walkers nor local businesses would stand for this. But given that any summer Saturday sees the Pen y Pass car park full up and hundreds of cars on the verges around Pen y Gwyrd, with their occupants obliged to traipse the dangerous A4086, we may see this idea returning soon, along with a really useful Sherpa service.

Pete's Eats, Llanberis

Accommodation and food

Tourist Information (general)
For local accommodation including the many hotels at Capel Curig, Betws y Coed, Beddgelert, Bangor and Caernarfon: Caernarfon TI, Oriel Pendeitsh, Castle St, Caernarfon LL55 1SE Tel. 01286 672232; Bangor TI, 2 Llys y Dderwen, Ffordd Gelli Morgan, Parc Menai, Bangor LL57 4BL Tel. 0870 1211251; Conwy Castle Visitor Centre, Rose Hill Street Conwy LL32 8LD Tel. 01492 592248

Youth Hostels
National Office: Trevelyan House, Dimple Rd, Matlock DE4 3YH; Central reservations Tel. 01629 592700 www.yha.org.uk

Camping
www.UKcampsite.co.uk

General Transport
All places here are on the Sherpa bus network – see 'Transport' above for those, and for rail links.

Pubs and cafés marked with asterisks * are the authors' own favourites.

Northern Carneddau

Tourist Information Conwy Tel. 01492 592248
Youth Hostels Rowen Tel. 0845 371 9038 grid ref SH747721 (summer only, with volunteer warden)
Conwy Tel. 0845 371 9732 grid ref SH775773 (year round)
Pubs *Ty Gwyn Hotel, Rowen is a splendid pub in the village centre serving excellent food

Llyn Ogwen

Youth Hostel Idwal Cottage Tel. 0845 371 9744 grid ref SH648604 (closed Jan - Mar and weekdays Nov, Dec)
Camping Gwern Gof Isaf (grid reference SH686601) all year 01690 720276; and Gwern Gof Uchaf (grid reference SH673603) Mar – Oct 01690 720294 www.tryfanwales.co.uk
Cafes snack bar at Ogwen Cottage

Llanberis and Nant Peris

Tourist Information Llanberis TIC (no voicemail and very helpful) 41b High St, Llanberis, Caernarfon LL55 4EU 01286 870765
Youth Hostel Tel. 0845 371 9645 grid ref SH574596 (Apr–Nov)
Independent hostels / bunkhouses bunkhouse at Heights Hotel Tel. 01286 871179 www.heightshotel.co.uk; Llwyn Celyn Bach, and Snowdon Inn – see camping (below)
Camping Nant Peris has several basic farm sites, including Blaen-y-nant in Llanberis Pass (grid ref SH623568)
Llanberis has Llwyn Celyn Bach, Capel Coch Road (near youth hostel) grid ref SH573595 Tel. 01286 870923 www.campinginllanberis.com March – October. At Cwm-y-glo there's Snowdon Inn grid ref SH554623 Tel. 01286 870289 www.thesnowdoninn.co.uk
Supplies general store, and Spar 7.00am – 11.00pm Mon-Sat; Joe Brown's gear shop; cash machine inside post office.
Pubs *Vaynol Arms, Nant Peris; *Royal Victoria Hotel, Llanberis; *Padarn Lake Hotel, Llanberis
Cafes *Pete's Eats, Llanberis (01286 870358) has been described as the best café in the world – a great chippy for big appetites, new climbs book, shower; *Pencuenant Isaf 17th-century tea rooms (01286 872606) on the Llanberis Path up Snowdon open 9am–9pm in summer – an excellent walker friendly licenced cafe with views of Llyn Padarn.
Local Transport Mon – Fri bus 86 to Bangor, also Caernarfon

Pen y Pass

Youth Hostel Tel. 0845 371 9534 grid ref SH647557 (all year)
Pubs *Pen-y-Gwryd Hotel, Nantgwynant – historic inn with good atmosphere.
Cafes Gorphwysfa Café at the car park open from 8.30am

Capel Curig

Youth Hostel Tel. 0845 371 9110 grid ref SH726578 (closed Dec and Jan)
Independent Hostels / bunkhouses bunkhouse, Bryn Tyrch farm (beside youth hostel) arrive in fours Tel. 01690 720414; Bryn Derwen bunk barn 01690 720312; above Capel Curig, Tal y Waun has an outhouse labelled bunkhouse.
Camping Bryn Tyrch farm beside youth hostel (see bunkhouses); Dolgam (grid ref SH743572) all year Tel. 01690 720228
Supplies Pinnacle Stores Capel Curig 8am - 6pm 01690 720201; three outdoor shops
Pubs Cobdens Hotel Tel. 01690 720223; Bryn Tyrch Tel. 01690 720243; Ty'n y Coed Tel. 01690 720331
Cafes *Pinnacle Café – large portions, closes 4.45pm 01690 720201

Nant Gwynant

Youth Hostel Bryn Gwynant Tel. 0845 371 9108 grid ref SH640513 (all year)
Independent hostels / bunkhouses Bryn Dinas bunkhouse, near foot of Watkin Path (grid ref SH625503) Tel. 01766 890646
Camping Hafod Y Llan (National Trust) caravan-free farm site (grid ref SH629514) Tel: 01766 510129; Llyn Gwynant Campsite grid ref SH651523 Tel: 01766 890 340 www.gwynant.com Easter to November
Cafes Gwynant Café at bottom of Watkin Path

Beddgelert

Tourist Information Canolfan Hebog, Beddgelert, Caernarfon, Gwynedd LL55 4YD Tel. 01766 890615
Camping Forest Holidays (grid ref SH577491) Tel. 0845 130 8224 year round; Cae Du (grid ref SH596486) March – Oct Tel. 01766 890345 www.caeducampsite.co.uk
Supplies Emrys House 01766 890240 open 9am–6pm, early closing Weds, 10am–5pm Sundays. (But shop currently for sale,

may close or hours may change.)
Pubs several
Cafes several; good ice cream bar
Local Transport from 2009 Beddgelert is now reached by the Welsh Mountain Railway, see above.

Rhyd-ddu

Youth Hostel Snowdon Ranger Tel. 0845 371 9659 grid ref SH565550
Independent Hostels / bunkhouses bunkhouse Cwellyn Arms has bunkhouse and barn: Pentre Bach (on A4085 west of Rhyd-ddu grid ref SH531579) Tel. 01286 650643 www.bachventures.co.uk (year round; also camping)
Camping Cwellyn Arms (campsite is up the road at Llyn Cwellyn) 01766 890321; Silver Birches camp site Betws y Garmon; Bryn Gloch camp site just north of Betws y Garmon
Pub *Cwellyn Arms – open '9 days a week' for good bar meals www.snowdoniainn.co.uk
Local Transport Welsh Mountain Railway, see above. For the Nantlle ridge, a taxi-bus can be ordered between Rhyd-ddu and Penygroes/Talysarn – phone Bws Gwyneth (above).

Organisations

Fell Runners Association
membership: Martin Stone, Sleagill Head Farm, Penrith CA10 3HD; www.fellrunner.org.uk

Long Distance Walkers' Association
Membership Secretary 7 Shetland Way, Radcliffe, Manchester, M26 4UH www.ldwa.org.uk

Rucksack Club Manchester-based but historically involved with the Welsh Threes, and with club hut, Beudy Mawr, at Nant Peris: www.rucksackclub.org

Gorphwysfa Mountaineering Club (organisers of 1000m Peaks Race) www.gorphwysfaclub.org.uk

1000 Metre Peaks Race
Entry forms and race regulations can be downloaded at www.gorphwysfaclub.org.uk, or are available from Mrs Jean

Hall, 81 Brook Street, Wymesfold, Loughborough, LE12 6TT jean.hall1@btinternet.com. Information can also be obtained from Harvey Lloyd harvey@richlloyd.fsnet.co.uk or for services entries (police, army etc) from: The Commandant, Capel Curig Training Camp, Betws-y-Coed, LL24 0AP

Useful Reading

The books marked 'out of print' are all available at sensible price second hand.

Classics

I Bought a Mountain – Thomas Firbank (Harrap, John Jones, and others 978-1-87108305-7 out of print) the classic work that inspired the 3000s challenge

Wild Wales George Borrow (Bridge Books 978-1-872424-98-9 currently out of print, available as free ebook online) pioneering guidebook of 1862, vigorous and opinionated

Backpacking in Wales Showell Styles (Hale 1977; 978-0-7091-5958-2 out of print)

Walking Guides

The Ridges of Snowdonia Steve Ashton (Cicerone 978-1-85284-350-2) more about feelings than footpaths, a very philosophical guidebook

Hillwalking in Snowdonia Steve Ashton (Cicerone 978-1-85284-349-6) 68 routes, with OS map extracts and fine photos

Hillwalking in Wales Vols 1 & 2 Peter Hermon (Cicerone 978-1-85284-081-5 / 082-2) the most complete guide to the mountains of Wales

Pictorial Guides to the Mountains of Snowdonia John Gillham (Frances Lincoln 2010) a new 4-volume series of almost everything there is out there

The Mountains of England and Wales Vol 1 Wales John and Anne Nuttall (Cicerone 978-1-85284-304-5) complete guide to everything over 2000ft (610m)

Mountain and Hillwalking in Snowdonia Carl Rogers (Mara Books) 2-volume series covering the 600m summits

Snowdonia Rocky Rambles Bryan Lynas (Sigma 978-1-85058-469-8 out of print) feet-on guide to the geology, in ten walks, cheerful and interesting

Rock Trails Snowdonia Paul Gannon (Pesda Press 978-1-906095-04-8) clear text and illustrations, with non-technical geology and ten rock-revealing mountain walks. Nicer looking than the Lynas book but less intellectually stimulating. Worth it for the exposition of Glyder cwms.

Long-distance and scrambling

A Welsh Coast to Coast John Gillham (Cicerone 978-1-85284-218-5 out of print) Snowdonia to Gower long-distance route with high-level and low-level alternatives, the basis for the Dragon's Back race route (Diadem 978-0906371275) out of print

Scrambles in Snowdonia Steve Ashton (Cicerone 978-1-85284-088-4) the definitive scrambling guide

Scrambles & Easy Climbs in Snowdonia Jon Sparks and others (Grey Stone 1 978-1-902017-01-3)

Across the Dragon's Back Ann Bowker's account of her walk over all the Welsh 2000s is at www.madaboutmountains.com

Glossary of Welsh Words

Aber	river mouth
Afon	river
Arddu	black crag
Bach/fach	small
Bedd	grave
Betws	chapel
Blaen	head of valley
Bryn	hill
Bwlch	pass, col, gap; spacebar (on keyboard)
Bws	bus
Cae	field
Caer	fort
Carnedd/garnedd	cairn
Capel	chapel
Carreg/garreg	stone
Castell	castle
Cefn	rounded ridge (literally, a back)
Clogwyn	cliff
Coch/goch	red
Coed	wood (plural of coeden: tree)
Cors/gors	bog

Craig	rock, crag
Crib	sharp ridge (literally, a comb)
Cwm	coomb, valley
Cwn	dog
Dinas	hill fort (or town)
Diolch	thank you
Du/ddu	black
Drws	door
Dwr	water
Dyffryn	valley
Eglwys	church
Esgair	ridge
Eryri	eagle's nest, eyrie; Snowdonia
Ffordd	way, road
Ffridd	enclosed grazing land
Ffynnon	spring
Glas/las	blue, green
Gwyn	white
Gwynt	wind
Hafod	high-altitude summer dwelling
Hendre	winter dwelling
Isaf	lowest
Llan	church or blessed place
Llwybr cyhoeddus	public foot-path
Llwyd	grey
Llyn	lake
Maen	stone

Maes	field/ meadow
Mawr/fawr	large
Melin/felin	mill
Moch	pigs (mochyn: pig)
Moel/foel	featureless hill (literally, bald)
Mynydd	mountain
Nant	stream
Ogof	cave
Pant	clearing, hollow
Pen	peak (literally, head)
Person	cascade
Plas	mansion
Pont/bont	bridge
Pwll	pool
Rhaeadr	waterfall
Rhyd	ford
Saeth(au)	arrow(s)
Troed	foot
Trum, drum	ridge
Twll	hole, cavern
Ty	house
Uchaf	uppermost
Waun (from gwaun)	moor
Wen (from gwyn)	white, silver, blessed
Wrach (from gwrach)	witch
Y, Yr	the
Ynys	island

A useful lexicon is at Cardiff University's www.cs.cf.ac.uk/fun/welsh/LexiconForms.html. If you insert an altered form (such as 'goch') it identifies the original ('coch').

Pronouncing Welsh
Unlike English, Welsh has logical spelling. If you can write a word down then, in theory, you can pronounce it. But not if you try to pronounce it like English! A few rules will let you pronounce Welsh so that a Welsh speaker could understand, though they may still laugh at you a bit...

Consonants:
C is always hard, like English "K" – Cefn "Kevun".
CH is as in Scots "Loch"
D is as in English but DD is a voiced "th" – like English 'Breathe" (rather than English "Breath").
F is like English "V" – Fach "Vach"; but FF is like English "F"
L is as in English but LL is a Scots "CH" followed by an "L" – Llyn "CHlun"

Vowels
U is pronounced as I in the south (Trum "trim") but is a more nondescript vowel in the north
W can be consonant or vowel. When working as a vowel, pronounced like "OO" in "Good". So Cwm "Coom"
Y can be consonant or vowel. When working as a vowel, pronounced like the nondescript sound at the end of 'Mother'. Y, the Welsh for 'the', sounds like "Uh!" I just got punched in the stomach.
Yr Wyddfa – "Ur Wuthva".

World's shortest conversational Welsh phrasebook

hello	sut mae
good morning	bore da
good afternoon	prynhawn da
good night	nos da
thank you	diolch
you're welcome	croeso
please	os gwelwch yn dda
one, two, three, four	un, dau, tri, pedwar
cup of coffee	dan o gofi
cup of tea	paned o de
cake	teisen

Mountain Rescue

To attract help: the international mountain distress signal by shouts, torch flashes, or whistle is six sounds/flashes spread over a minute, followed by one minute without signals. The reply is three signals spread over a minute, followed by one minute without signals. As not every hill-goer knows this signal, SOS (dot dot dot dash dash dash dot dot dot) or a simple cry of 'Help!' can also be used.

Being lost or benighted in normal or moderately poor weather are not in themselves sufficient reason for calling for rescue.

To contact Mountain Rescue by phone:

from a land line – dial 999

from a mobile phone – dial 999 or 112: this will connect you using any available network, and may work even if your phone shows 'no signal'. If you can't get through, try moving a few steps, possibly onto or off a summit or ridge crest.

When you get through, ask the emergency operator for North Wales Police.

THE END